GREAT SOURCE

WriteTraits

Student Traitbook

Vicki Spandel and Jeff Hicks

GREAT
SOURCE.

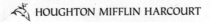

HOUGHTON MIFFLIN HARCOURT

www.greatsource.com
800-289-4490

Acknowledgements

For permission to reprint copyrighted material, grateful acknowledgement is made to the following sources:

Excerpt from *Crazy Loco* by David Rice. Text copyright © 2001 by David Rice. Reprinted by permission of Dial Books, for Young Readers, a division of Penguin Young Readers Group, a member of Penguin group (USA) Inc.

Excerpt from *G is for Googol: A Math Alphabet Book* by David M. Schwartz. Text copyright © 1998 by David M. Schwartz. Reprinted by permission of Tricycle Press, an imprint of Random House Children's Books, a division of Random House, Inc.

Excerpt from *Hope Was Here* by Joan Bauer. Text © 2000 by Joan Bauer. Reprinted by permission of G.P. Putnam's Sons, a division of Penguin Young Readers Group, a member of Penguin Group (USA) Inc. and Sterling Lord Literistic, Inc.

Excerpt from *Leaving Home* by Sneed B. Collard III. Text copyright © 2002 by Sneed B. Collard III. Reprinted by permission of Houghton Mifflin Harcourt Publishing Company.

Excerpt from *Lives of the Artists: Comedies, Tragedies (and What the Neighbors Thought)* by Kathleen Krull. Text copyright © 1994 by Kathleen Krull. Reprinted by permission of Houghton Mifflin Harcourt Publishing Company and Writer's House, LLC., on behalf of the author.

Excerpt from *Stowaway* by Karen Hesse. Text copyright © 2000 by Karen Hess. Reprinted by permission of Margaret K. McElderry Books, an imprint of Simon & Schuster Children's Publishing Division.

Excerpt from *Stuck in Neutral* by Terry Trueman. Text copyright © 2000 by Terry Trueman. Reprinted by permission of HarperCollins Publishers.

ISBN-13 978-0-669-01517-1

ISBN-10 0-669-01517-2

1 2 3 4 5 6 7 8 9 10 1409 18 17 16 15 14 13 12 11 10

4500237787

About the Authors

Jeff Hicks

Jeff taught for 18 years in the Beaverton School District (home of the 6-traits) where he enjoyed working with students to help them find their voices as writers. He is the co-author of *Write Traits Classroom Kits*, *Write Traits Advanced*, and *Write Traits Kindergarten*. Though his heart is still in the classroom, he is now a full-time writer, presenter, and professional development consultant. He lives in Beaverton with his wife and son, and he currently serves on the Beaverton School Board.

Vicki Spandel

Vicki is a founding coordinator of the 17-member teacher team that developed the original, nationally recognized 6-trait model for writing assessment and instruction. A specialist in teaching writing and revision to students of all ages, she is the author of *Write Traits Classroom Kits*, *Write Traits Advanced*, and *Write Traits Kindergarten*, as well as *The 9 Rights of Every Writer*, *Creating Writers*, and *Creating Young Writers*. She makes her home in the town of Sisters, Oregon, bordering the beautiful Three Sisters Wilderness.

Contents

UNIT 4: WORD CHOICE

UNIT 5: SENTENCE FLUENCY

Ideas

Whether you are writing a fictional story about a flying dog or a factual report on fire ants in Australia, the trait of **Ideas** is all about providing information to readers—in just the right quantity. Too many unneeded details will bog readers down, making it hard to stay focused on your message. Skimpy details leave questions unanswered and suggest that you, the writer, didn't do your research. The secret is balance. If you begin with a clear sense of direction and gather enough information to know your topic well, readers will feel educated, entertained, or both. Then they'll want to read the next thing you write.

In this unit, you'll focus on several strategies that can help bring balance to your writing. In the lessons that follow, you'll have a chance to

- define your topic.
- "defog" writing to make meaning clear.
- use details to create a vivid character sketch.
- cut unnecessary details, or filler.

Name _____   Date _____

Sample Paper 1

Score for Ideas _____

My Most Scary Experience

Last week we were skiing in this really neat place. We were really racing down the slopes, and I got going too fast on one of the turns. I was trying to keep up with my brother, Matt, who is a big show-off. He shows off all the time, and it's so irritating. Like last year we were on the same baseball team because our school only has one team. We both play outfield, and I ran to catch this really high fly ball. Matt ran for it too, and we were each staring up into the sun. He bumped into me on purpose (even though he said it was an accident—yeah, right) so he could make the catch and show the coach what a great player he is.

So back to the skiing thing. This time he could not bump into me because he was in front. He was going so fast he was a blur. My mom would have had a fit! She hates for us to take chances. Personally, I wish Matt would take even more chances so he would get grounded forever! How great would that be?

I came around this one turn. I was trying to follow Matt's tracks, and maybe I was. I couldn't even tell anymore, he was kicking up so much snow. I came so close to this one huge tree that I missed it by only about two inches. It almost, well in fact it did, scrape one of my gloves. If I had hit that tree I probably wouldn't even be here. At the very least, it would have knocked me out. That was my most scary experience ever.

Sample Paper 2

Score for Ideas _____

How to Leave a Phone Message

My parents both work, so I am assigned the job of taking phone messages. I know what you're thinking. Why don't his parents get an answering machine? Why don't they just use cell phones? Well see, those would be simple solutions. We're not into simple here at our house. We're all about responsibility—especially if it has to do with me. If there's the tiniest opportunity for me to learn anything involving responsibility, my parents leap on it like it's gold. So I'm sitting here with my phone pad, all ready, and I have some tips for people who might be thinking of phoning us.

First, when you are leaving a message, give your name and spell it. Spell slowly. Don't just say, "Hi, this is Darnaldo." This is actually one of my dad's friends. He spelled his name the first time he called, but he's one of those spellers that gives you sample words—"d" as in desperate, "a" as in "aardvark." Give me a break. I forget what I am supposed to be writing and I wind up writing *Desperate Aardvark.*

Second, speak slowly—especially when giving your phone number. And keep in mind that phone numbers have a rhythm: three numbers, then four. They all go like that. Trust me. But some people give their numbers like this: 5 (pause) 558435. You know what? That's not your number. Your number is 555 (pause) 8435. Hear the difference? Of course, I can always ask the person to repeat, but that's harder than it sounds. Here's the thing. If the person taking the message asks you a question, listen! That means you have to stop talking. Phones aren't like being together. That's an illusion. You're not together. Only one person at a time can talk. There's no lip reading on the phone. Gestures don't help either.

Somewhere, far in the future, my parents will purchase cell phones. I dream of this all the time. They'll even learn to text. I'm confident of it. I'll tell them it's their responsibility. Meanwhile, follow these tips, and you might even get your call returned (especially if you're not phoning us).

Ideas

The WRITER...
makes everything crystal clear,
beginning to end.

So the READER...
_____
_____
_____

The WRITER...
keeps the writing small
and focused.

So the READER...
_____
_____
_____

The WRITER...
chooses details with care.

So the READER...
_____
_____
_____

The WRITER...
knows the topic inside and out.

So the READER...
_____
_____
_____

Defining Your Topic

The first question most writers ask is, "What shall I write about?" And the first answer to this is usually a broad topic relating to the writer's interests: travel, sports, animals, and so on. As you know, however, big topics can be unwieldy. Good writers narrow their topics, bringing them down to manageable size and turning a topic like *sports,* for example, into *baseball* . . . then *pitching* . . . then *three ways to strike out a good hitter.* In this lesson, we'll work on narrowing big topics, along with two more steps important in defining a topic: (1) writing a good thesis statement (a summary of your main idea) and (2) posing three writers' questions to answer in your writing. Completing these steps will put you in an excellent position to begin a rough draft.

Step 1: Going from Big to Focused

Below are four writing topics. See if you can put them in order from biggest (1) to most focused, narrow, and specific (4).

As you order them, think like a **reader:** Would this make one chapter, or a whole book? Then like a **writer:** How long would it take to research this?

_____ Rock and Roll

_____ Comparing Styles of Two Rock and Roll Drummers

_____ Music

_____ Rock and Roll Drumming

Share and Compare

Meet with a partner to compare your rankings. Did they match? One more question: Is the final topic (the one you marked 4) narrow enough? If not, can you make it even more focused? If you can, write your new topic here:

_____

Your Turn to Shrink a Topic

Working with a partner, choose a BIG topic of your own or work with one from our list. Narrow it down in stages, making it smaller and smaller until it's a good size to research and write about.

Possible BIG topics:

- Sports
- Dancing
- Animals
- Food

Our BIG topic is _____

Narrower _____

Still narrower _____

Narrow enough _____

Are the following statements true of your final topic?

☐ Our topic is small enough to research easily.

☐ Our topic is small enough to write about easily.

Step 2: Writing a Thesis

A thesis is a statement that sums up your main message. Sometimes it's the first sentence in your writing—but it doesn't have to be.

What's the difference between a thesis and a topic? Simple: A topic is a **word or phrase** describing the main subject the writer will focus on. A thesis is a **sentence** that shows purpose and direction. Following are some examples.

Topic: Cats

Thesis: Cats are harder to train than dogs.

Topic: Food

Thesis: Eating a vegetarian diet can improve your health.

With your partner (or writing circle), come up with a thesis statement for each of these topics.

Topic: Driving

Thesis: _____

Topic: Seventh grade

Thesis: _____

Turning Your Topic into a Thesis

Look back at the narrow topic you and your partner (or writing circle) thought of in **Step 1: Going from Big to Focused**. Chances are, you didn't write it as a sentence—yet. Turn it into a thesis by doing that now.

Remember that a thesis is a complete sentence and sums up your main message.

Our thesis:

_____

_____

Step 3: Identifying the Top 3

As you know, good writers think like readers. And now here's your chance. Look back at your thesis. Now imagine that one of your readers read that thesis. What are the Top 3 questions that a reader would want you to answer in your writing? Think hard. With your partner, write your questions here:

1. _____

2. _____

3. _____

Hang on to the questions you just wrote. You will need them for the next step.

Share and Compare

Meet in a writing circle with two writers who have NOT seen your thesis—or your three questions. Follow these steps:

1. Share your thesis aloud with the other writers. (Do NOT share your three questions!)

2. Listen carefully as they share their theses.

3. With your own partner, write down the three questions you want the other team to answer in their paper. Be thoughtful and creative.

4. Exchange questions.

5. Compare sets of questions. Based on your thesis, what questions did the other team think of? Based on your thesis, what questions did you and your partner think of?

As you compare the sets of questions, which of these is true?

☐ Our questions were identical!

☐ Our questions were different, and we like our own questions best.

☐ Our questions were different, and we like their questions!

☐ Our questions were different, and we like some of each. Both teams had good ideas!

Look over questions from both teams, and put a star beside the Top 3.

Name _____   Date _____

The 12-Minute Skeleton Draft

Are we serious?! We are! Yes, you can do a sketchy rough draft in about 12 minutes using the information you already have from this lesson. We'll call it a skeleton draft. It won't be complete, but it will have the following.

- A lead
- A design
- Enough information to plan your research
- A title

Go ahead, amaze yourself. Just follow these steps, using your own scratch paper.

1. Look at your thesis statement. Add some fascinating detail (maybe a new sentence or two) and turn it into a lead. You have **two minutes.**

2. Look at your Top 3 readers' questions—the ones you starred. Number them in the order in which you would answer them. Skip five lines after your lead and write the first question. Skip five more lines and write the second. Skip five more and write the third. You have **four minutes.**

3. Write two possible titles for this piece, and choose the one you like better. You have **two minutes.**

4. Use your remaining **four minutes** to think about how you will find answers to each reader's question. Under the question, jot down one of these options:

   - Know this (you know enough to answer this question yourself)
   - Interview _____ (fill in a name)
   - Internet (you'll look online for information)
   - Book (you'll check a book or similar resource)

Time's up, but guess what? You finished a rough draft *and* a research plan in less than 12 minutes. Not bad.

Name _____   Date _____

A Writer's Question

In this lesson, you created a skeleton draft for a piece you might never finish. But let's say you did. As you began writing, how much do you think your draft or your plan would change?

Putting It to the Test

You're taking a writing test and responding to a prompt you don't like very well. You cannot think what to say, or where to begin. How could the ideas from this lesson help you get started and help you write something the reader will respond to? (Remember, if you sound bored, the reader will be bored, too.)

Cutting Through the Fog

In places like San Francisco or London, people say the fog is sometimes as thick as pea soup. Mystery writers love it. Ocean fog is common, too. That's why lighthouses flash their beacons to help ships find their way. Actually, you don't have to visit London or cruise the sea to encounter fog. It can seep right into your own classroom in the form of vague writing. A lighthouse won't help you. But a good editor's pen will.

Sharing an Example: *Stuck in Neutral*

Clear, focused writing is like a welcome sign. It says, "Come right in, Reader! Look around, meet everybody, join in the conversation, laugh, cry, and learn!" Read the following passage from *Stuck in Neutral* by Terry Trueman. Ask yourself whether this writer put out the welcome sign.

I am in a wheelchair. I can't talk. I can't control my eyes in any way that does me any good, like to read a book or something. First off, I can't hold the book or turn the pages, but even if I could use my hands, my eyes go where they want to go; I can't control them. A lot of the time, luckily, my eyes do focus on stuff and manage to soak up what they're looking at. But it's like my eyes have little minds of their own—I can't will them to pay attention. One second I'll be looking at something and the next moment my eye muscles will decide that the smudge on the wall is where I should be looking, and that'll be that.

I do know how to read; my sister, Cindy, taught me when I was seven years old. I'd sit there . . . and Cindy would play . . . Teacher of the Year. She'd point to letters and sound them out, show me simple sentences, reading the words slowly, like her teacher must have once read them to her. When I'd flip around and vocalize . . . she'd scold me and then repeat her lessons. Cindy was playing. I was learning. I picked up reading from Cindy playing school with me, and through remembering sounds, and listening to words spoken as I saw them written down, like on TV screens, video credits, and in real life, from signs of every type, like MOTEL, which taught me m-o-t-e-l, to STOP, which taught me s-t-o-p. Reading is easy once you catch on that every letter just stands for a sound. . . Of course, nobody knows I can read. Like the captain says in Cool Hand Luke, "What we have here is a failure to communicate." In my case that's kind of like calling the Grand Canyon a pothole.

Stuck in Neutral
by Terry Trueman

Reflection

As a reader, did you feel the author told you enough to invite you right inside the character's experience? Write a sentence or two about how the passage made you feel, what it made you see in your mind, or anything else you want to say. Prepare to share your thoughts in a writing circle.

_____

_____

_____

What Did You Learn?

What did you learn about the narrator from this passage? What did you learn about his sister Cindy?

In your writing circle, divide up the work so that one or two of you focus on the narrator, and one or two focus on Cindy. Then follow these steps:

1. Read the passage again. Underline parts that tell something important about your character.

2. Write down three or four things you learned about your character:

   _____

   _____

   _____

   _____

   _____

Share and Compare

In your writing circles, discuss what you learned about the narrator and Cindy. Feel free to add more to your list. Then, discuss how you learned each thing. Did the author give you **specific details** that told you something about the character? Or did you make an **inference,** a best guess based on what you knew? Look back at your list of things you learned. Mark each one "D" for *Detail* or "I" for *Inference.*

Fog Alert!

Terry Trueman writes in a highly detailed way—as you probably noticed. What if he didn't, though? What if he let the fog just roll on in, right over his writing? Maybe it would look more like this (with apologies to Mr. Trueman):

> I'm kind of different from other people. I can't
> talk. I can't control my eyes. I know how to read.
> My sister showed me.

Obviously, our revision has fewer words. But what else is missing? You have four minutes to make a list, working with your partner or in a writing circle.

What's missing from this foggy version?

1. _____

2. _____

3. _____

4. _____

5. _____

6. _____

(If you think of more, keep going! Use scratch paper!)

Reflection

On a scale of 1 to 10, with 1 being NO CHANCE and 10 being A SURE THING, how likely would you be to keep reading a piece that began with the foggy version?

| 1 | 2 | 3 | 4 | 5 | 6 | 7 | 8 | 9 | 10 |

How likely is it you'll check out Terry Trueman's actual book, *Stuck in Neutral?*

1	2	3	4	5	6	7	8	9	10

Defogging

Following are three examples of foggy writing. Read all three. Then choose the one you think you can best defog. Read it again, pencil in hand, inserting notes, new words, questions, anything that will help you revise with power. When you finish, compose a new version on scratch paper or on the computer (if you have computer access). Your new version will probably be longer, but length is not the goal. *Detail* is the goal.

Example 1

A Trip

It was our third day of vacation, and the weather wasn't that great. We couldn't do a lot of the stuff we wanted to do. The food was uninteresting, and television was pretty yucky. My mom wanted to play the same board game over and over. It was hard to stay awake.

Example 2

The Neighbor's Pet

Our neighbors got this new pet. It's pretty cute and everything, but it's a lot of trouble to take care of. It spends a lot of time at our house—doing things it isn't supposed to do. I'm supposed to watch out for our new visitor. This eats up a lot of time. Oh, well.

Name .... Date ....

Example 3

The School Bully

If you've ever been bothered by a bully, then you know it is not a good experience. It makes you feel bad. In fact, you feel really bad. I get a lot of advice, but some of the people who give advice are not having the experience right now. I'm not sure they really know how it feels. It doesn't feel good. You want it to stop.

Share and Compare

Meet with a partner or in a writing circle to share your revisions. Who did an outstanding job of defogging? What was that writer's strategy?

A Writer's Question
Good writers notice small details: the way a deer's ears twitch at the slightest sound, how a character's hair falls, the way wind flattens the grass. Look back at the revision you just did. Is there a detail you noticed and wrote about that not everyone would notice? Underline it.

Putting It to the Test
Writers often wind up writing in a foggy way because they cave in to the temptation to use foggy language. What are some foggy words you should definitely omit from any on-demand essay?

From Sketch to Portrait

Have you ever watched a sketch artist work—maybe at a carnival or state fair? They're all about speed. They take one hasty look at the subject and go to work. Of course, they don't capture *every detail.* In fact, many people hardly recognize themselves in the final drawing. What if the artist took time to get to know you and look closely at your eyes, your smile, your hair, your posture, and the shrug of your shoulders? The result would be more of a true portrait.

Like sketchy drawing, sketchy writing leaves the reader with a mere hint of the person behind the words. To give your readers more, you need to capture the small details. A character that is real in your mind can become real on paper.

Sharing an Example: *Lives of the Writers*

Do you recognize the name E.B. White? As you may recall, he is the author of *Charlotte's Web* and *Stuart Little.* But even if you've read those books, you may not know much about him. Here is a short passage from the book *Lives of the Writers* by Kathleen Krull. As you read it, ask yourself, "What is E.B. White like? What am I learning about this writer?"

"Hello, Eileen? This is Elwyn White." He had practiced this greeting so many times that when the mother of the girl he wanted to date answered the phone instead of the girl herself, he was unable to change the words. How embarrassing! Eileen still went out with him, for as nervous and uncomfortable as Elwyn Brooks White could be, he was charming, too.

The youngest of six children, White (always called Andy after college) had a happy, secure childhood. He grew up to be a private person who lived just the way he wanted to, once he figured out what that was. As a young man he sold roach powder, played the piano, tried being a reporter (though writing about murders made him ill), and drove a Model T Ford (named Hotspur, for a character from a Shakespeare play) across the country.

Lives of the Writers: Comedies, Tragedies
(and What the Neighbors Thought)
by Kathleen Krull

Reflection

Look through the passage for clues that tell you something about E.B. White. See if you can list three things.

1. _____

2. _____

3. _____

How would you rate Krull's passage from 1 to 10?

1 = A barebones sketch with almost no information. I could have made this up.

10 = A true portrait—an insider's look at White. I feel I know him.

| 1 | 2 | 3 | 4 | 5 | 6 | 7 | 8 | 9 | 10 |

Sketches or Portraits?

Take a look at the following three writing examples. They are all written in first person, so the character is the person talking. Read each one, and decide whether the piece is so sketchy that you would say "Forget it!" and stop reading or so clear that you would say "Frame it!" and keep reading.

> Example 1

Cancel the Award Shows

When the Oscars or Grammys are on, count on me to switch channels—or just go read a book. I *love* movies and music, but I don't care to watch actors and musicians fawning over each other, crying phony tears, and thanking endless lists of lawyers and agents. Most of them look like they got their outfits from my little sister's dress-up box. And who does their hair? Someone without a brush or comb, obviously. If you ask me, these people need to spend less time congratulating each other and more time working at their craft.

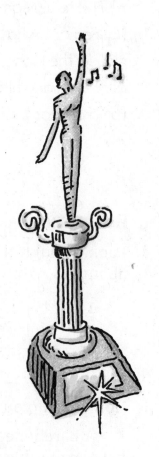

☐ Sketchy! I can't tell *anything* about this person.

☐ I get a hint or two—but there's not a strong personality yet.

☐ I know this person! It's a strong self-portrait.

Example 2

Oh, Great—Testing Time Again

It's that time of year again at school—state testing! They expect us to come back from our vacation all ready to sit down and take test after test. Testing in the morning. Testing in the afternoon. I'm still thinking about the great time I had on my vacation. I wish I were still on vacation! I don't want to look bad, so I will do my best. That doesn't mean I have to like it, though. If you want to know the truth, I'm sick of tests.

☐ Sketchy! I can't tell *anything* about this person.

☐ I get a hint or two—but there's not a strong personality yet.

☐ I know this person! It's a strong self-portrait.

Example 3

Rain

It rained again today. I'm pretty sure it rained yesterday, too. My team doesn't have practice when it rains. Some people don't like rain all that much. It can be OK, though. The grass greens up when it rains and you see more flowers. There is rain in the forecast for tomorrow, I think.

☐ Sketchy! I can't tell *anything* about this person.

☐ I get a hint or two—but there's not a strong personality yet.

☐ I know this person! It's a strong self-portrait.

Name _____   Date _____

Creating Your Own Portrait

Here's a chance to create a portrait of your own. Remember, detail is the key! Choose someone you know well: a relative, friend—even yourself! Your character does not have to be human (think of Charlotte from *Charlotte's Web*). And if you feel like your imagination is in high gear today, you can even make up a character, but be warned: It is a bit harder to make an invented character realistic.

HINT: Think about whether you prefer to write in first or third person.

Prewrite by drawing a sketch, listing details, or doing anything you find helpful. Then write for at least 15 minutes, using every other line so you can go back later to add details you forgot as you were writing. Make your portrait as vivid as you can. Make your character real and imagine how he or she feels.

Share and Compare

In your writing circles, share your character portraits and rate each other, using the same 1 to 10 scale you used to rank Krull's piece, *Lives of the Writers.* Choose one to share aloud with the whole class.

1	2	3	4	5	6	7	8	9	10

A barebones sketch   A true portrait

A Writer's Question

Our sketches were written in first person and did not include any physical detail about the speakers. Look back at the sketches and ask yourself, "Who do I picture in my mind?" Discuss this with your writing circles or your class. Try to figure out whether each speaker is male or female, how old the speaker is, and what he or she looks like. Then see if you can pinpoint the specific clues that tell you these things. If you cannot picture the person and have no idea who he or she is, what does that tell you about the writing?

Putting It to the Test

From this lesson, you discovered that vivid writing creates a kind of portrait of the person speaking. As you are writing in an on-demand situation, what sort of portrait are you creating? Who will your readers picture as they read your writing?

Packing Only What You Need

When you are packing your backpack for school, you don't stick a couple bricks in there just for the heck of it. It's heavy enough, right? You also want to leave out the **filler** when you write. Filler does just what its name suggests—it fills space that should go to more important details. Let's say you're reading a friend's paper about her trip to Orlando. Do you want to hear what time the plane took off, what color socks she wore, or what brand of toothpaste she used? Or would you rather hear about the pool with the 350-foot water slide and the live alligator she saw right in the parking lot? Exactly. Whether you're traveling or writing, pack only what you need.

Sharing an Example: *Stowaway*

Following is a passage from Karen Hesse's book *Stowaway*. It's an entry from the journal of character Nicholas Young, who has paid some crewmen to help him stow away on the ship *Endeavour*.

Read the passage aloud, quietly. Does Nick give us the details we need to feel part of his experience? Or does he overload us with a lot of filler?

WEDNESDAY 31st TO THURSDAY 1st SEPTEMBER [*Lat. 44° 56' N, Long. 9° 9' W*] All day the sea rose, breaking over the deck. Captain had the men everywhere in the rigging, trying to save the ship from being torn to pieces by the wind.

Just before first watch the Bosun staggered to the side and shook his fist at the sea, cursing it for stealing his skiff. But ship's cook, Mr. Thompson, was angrier still. A dozen of his hens drowned in the storm. Mr. Thompson kept muttering how he was never to feed the entire Company if the sea kept killing his livestock. I'd never seen ship's cook so close before. He has but one hand!

The storm, at last, is blown out and *Endeavour* floats easy in the sea again. The servant boy, John Charlton, comes past when he can, leaving bits to eat. He also brings with him good cheer with that kind face of his and that beaming smile. I don't know much about him but that he is from London, has a friendly nature, and at fifteen years of age has spent his last three years at sea. He says my red hair reminds him of his mother. He knows his way about, John Charlton does, and he knows the men who brought me aboard. They can be trusted, he said. They're good men.

Stowaway
by Karen Hesse

Name _____ Date _____

Identifying Important Details

Read the passage again, looking for places where Nick reveals important information. In the circle below, jot down important, helpful details Nick shares with readers. Outside the circle, write anything you think is filler.

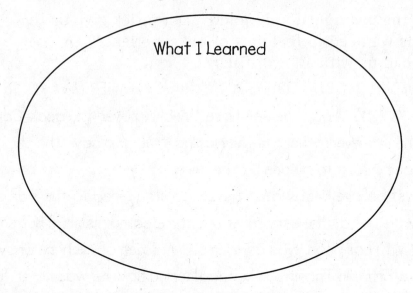

What I Learned

Share and Compare

Meet with a partner or in a writing circle to share your responses. Discuss what you learn from this passage about the following.

- Nick
- John Charlton
- The Bosun
- The ship *Endeavour*
- Life aboard the ship

Did everyone agree on what was useful and what was filler? If you were author Karen Hesse's editor, what would you say about the amount of detail?

☐ Too much filler! Cut!

☐ Not enough! Sketchy!

☐ Just right! Each detail counts.

Hey! No Fair Peeking!

Filler can be very distracting. Let us show you. Here's the passage from *Stowaway* with just a bit of filler added (apologies to the author). Read this version with a highlighter or pencil in your hand. **Without looking back at the author's original,** highlight or cross out the filler.

Just before first watch the Bosun staggered to the side and shook his fist at the sea, cursing it for stealing his skiff. The Bosun had a red hat that he pulled down over his ears. It looked like it would keep him warm. But ship's cook, Mr. Thompson, was angrier still. A dozen of his hens drowned in the storm. There were white, brown, and black chickens. They all had names too, poor things. Mr. Thompson kept muttering how he was never to feed the entire Company if the sea kept killing his livestock. Well, no kidding! Now they'd be eating potatoes for every meal. I'd never seen ship's cook so close before. He has but one hand! He didn't have a wooden leg or anything, though.

Reflection

How easy was it to spot the filler?

- [ ] It was a snap! I could spot it a mile away.
- [ ] I had to think about it. I'm not positive I got it right.
- [ ] I couldn't tell any difference between the two versions because this one sounded pretty much like the original.

Filler, Beware!

Here's a piece of writing for you to revise on your own. Read it through once to get a sense of what it's about. Then, read it again, pencil in hand, and when you spot filler, draw a single line through it. **HINT:** Sometimes shortening a sentence is enough.

The Winter Olympics

For the first time in my life, I really watched the Winter Olympics. Well, I watched most of it. I didn't watch, like, every second of it or anything. I'm not really a fan of figure skating, so I avoided those events like the plague. I really did not watch much figure skating at all. The speed skating was thrilling, however. I also loved the cross-country skiing races. Many countries were represented. Over 150 countries were represented. The event was a great blend of traditional winter sports and new events from the world of extreme sports. The announcers were always wearing sweaters and sitting in what looked like somebody's living room. It had some big, comfortable looking chairs and this neat fireplace with a fire going all the time. One event, the skeleton, made its return after being dropped years ago. It fit right in with the luge and bobsled, two of my all-time favorites. They also featured many great human-interest stories. A number of athletes were trying for big comebacks after terrible injuries. Some competitors were trying to break records for the total number of individual medals. It seems like the host country always wins a lot of medals. Not every country won medals, of course. Some countries only won one or two medals. A few athletes won no medals but, because of their efforts, still won the hearts of all the fans. It looked like the crowds were huge. The competitors had a nice place to stay. If I were an athlete, I wouldn't mind being in the Olympics!

Share and Compare

Meet with a partner and compare revisions. Did you cross out the same parts? (It's OK to cross out more as you discuss the passage.) Which one of the following statements comes closest to describing your revision?

☐ We hardly crossed out a thing!

☐ We crossed out a few lines.

☐ We crossed out half or more!

What additional details does this piece need now that you have found and removed the filler? With your partner, go back and insert a caret (∧) each place you think the writer needs to add information.

You've done Steps 1 and 2 on our list. If you were the writer, what would be Step 3?

1. Cross out filler (check)

2. Identify spots that need more detail (check)

3. _____

A Writer's Question

Let's say you look at a piece of your own writing and discover that it has filler. Does that mean you did something wrong? Or is filler a natural part of drafting? Do all writers include filler in their work at some point, or do really good writers only write good stuff? Does filler serve any purpose?

Putting It to the Test

In a testing situation, you might not have a lot of time to go back and cross out any filler you find. What little strategies can you use to keep filler to a minimum?

Conventions & Presentation

The WRITER...
edits everything thoroughly.

So the READER...
_____
_____
_____

The WRITER...
looks <u>and</u> listens for errors.

So the READER...
_____
_____
_____

The WRITER...
uses conventions to bring out meaning and voice.

So the READER...
_____
_____
_____

The WRITER...
is thoughtful about presentation.

So the READER...
_____
_____
_____

Conventions and Presentation
Editing Level 1: Conventions
Making Editing Manageable

When faced with a job that seems really BIG—a report on your state's history, an essay on a 1,000-page novel, cleaning your garage—it's easy to feel overwhelmed. You're not sure where to begin, and you can't imagine finishing. Many writers feel this way about editing. They've already worked so hard doing their research and getting a draft on paper. And then, there's more! Checking the spelling, grammar, punctuation, usage, paragraphing . . . Does this list ever end? Our best advice is to break editing down into several small jobs. Taking things step by step is one good way to make any big task manageable.

A Warm-Up

Here's a step-by-step guide that makes editing simpler to handle. Read the whole thing through and decide how much or how little you want to do at one time. Either way, you get a full minute for each step.

Editing Guide

Step 1: Read the passage for <u>meaning.</u>

Step 2: Edit carefully for <u>spelling errors.</u>

Step 3: Edit carefully for <u>punctuation errors.</u>

Step 4: Edit carefully for errors in <u>grammar.</u>

Step 5: Edit for <u>repeated or missing words.</u>

HINT: Carefully reading a passage before doing any editing helps your brain size up the job and begin working subconsciously. (And that's a good thing.)

i just dont get the whether around hear. yesterday, it was 84

dgrees and today it chili and raining Spring weather can be be so

confusing around here I gess that's why they say, "if you don't

like the weather, weight five minutes" It's probably also why their's

a whole Chanel devoted just the weather

HINT: Go back through the passage one more time, pencil in hand. Give yourself a gold star (just in your mind) if you find even one error you missed. Most editors do!

Share and Compare

Compare your editing results with a partner's by counting the number of errors you each found. Do your totals match? Your teacher will share the number of errors in the passage so you know if you missed anything.

Sharpening the Old Editor's Eye

Here are four short writing examples for you to edit. As you go through the examples, you'll be asked to look for a little more each time. This gradual increase in difficulty helps train your editor's eyes and ears to see and hear more and more. Use the following guidelines.

- Read aloud, slowly, so you do not miss anything.
- Have a writing handbook or other resources handy so you can check things out.
- Use the correct marks from the copyeditor's poster.
- Go back for one more look to be sure you didn't miss anything.

Example 1

Editing Focus: Spelling

What a bussy weekend! My parents piked my bother and me up from school early on Friday, so what we cud fyl to St. Louis for a family wedding in Satruday.

Example 2

Editing Focus: Spelling; capitals to start sentences; punctuation to end sentences

my oldest cuzin, the one getting maried, asked my brother and me to be the ring barers this happened onec before when i was littel back then I thogt I was going to be a "ring bear," so I asked my mom if I could be a Grizzly Bear?

Example 3

Editing Focus: Spelling; capitalization; punctuation; grammar

my brother and me are only abut a Year apart we look alot like twins my cousin thought therefore that weed look cute in maching tuxedoes with tails and top hats achually, we did look pretty good, but black tuxedos on a hot day was pretty uncomftorble, expecially during the long photo shoot befor the Wedding

Example 4

Editing Focus: Spelling; capitals; punctuation; missing or repeated words; EVERYTHING!

i can't weight to see the pitcher were they posed all the Guys in Tuxedos wearring cool sunglasses it it was hard because we wasn't suppose to smile everyone's freinds was taking pictures at the the same time for a moment it felt as though we were fameous people at press Conference but then I could feel the swet dripping down my back all i wanted rite then was to get to get into some reglar close

Share and Compare

Compare your editing of each example with a partner's. Did you find the same errors and the same number of errors? If your partner found something you missed or used a copyeditor's symbol you had forgotten, mark those changes on your paper, too. Then coach your teacher as he or she models the editing of each passage.

A Writer's Questions

When you're writing on a computer, you have spell check and grammar check to help you. Is that enough? If it's not enough, why bother with it at all?

Getting to Know You (in a Nutshell)

Most people are curious about other people's lives and love looking for details from magazines, websites, blogs, and TV programs. Whole sections of library and bookstore shelves are filled with biographies—books about people's lives.

A good biography is the result of in-depth research and extensive interviews with the person (if alive), relatives, friends, coworkers, classmates, and the husband or wife. Bio authors strive to hunt for informational tidbits curious readers might want to know, without being too intrusive.

Writers who create author bios for book jackets have another challenge. They have to fit all this fascinating information (usually with a photo) into a small space. Book bios often run less than 100 words. That's not much copy in which to sum up a person's life! But author bios, even short ones, serve an important purpose. Getting to know the person behind the words can enrich your reading experience and help you understand the author's point of view. Suppose YOU wrote a book. What would you want your bio to say?

A Warm-Up

Take time to look at some author bios. You may wish to look at the inside back panels of various book jackets. Or you can do an online search. Many websites offer biographical information on authors.

Your focus here is not on collecting specific details about particular authors. Instead, ask yourself what kinds of information does a good bio usually seem to include? What makes an author bio informative or just plain fun to read? With your partner or in a writing circle, make a list of various things you think should appear in a well-written bio.

HINT: Don't forget visuals!

"Must-Include" Information for Author Bios:

1. _____
2. _____
3. _____
4. _____
5. _____
6. _____
7. _____
8. _____
9. _____
10. _____

Share and Compare

Discuss your lists as a class. If someone mentions an important feature you didn't think of, add it to your list.

Whittling a Bio Down to Size

Following is a very rough draft of an author bio for a book that's almost ready to go to print. The editor needs an expert to revise it. With your partner or writing circle, review your list of things included in strong bios. Then review the editor's notes for this book: title, genre, intended audience, and length requirement. (The current rough draft runs 226 words.) As you revise, feel free to cut copy, change the order, or add details. You can suggest any visuals you think are needed.

HINT: Don't forget to do a final word count!

Editor's Notes for Samantha R. Connors

Book Title: *The Silver Sword of Sammarrkahn Trilogy, Part One*

Author: Samantha R. Connors

Genre: Fantasy Adventure

Target Audience: Ages 12–15

Maximum Word Count: 100 words

Samantha R. Connors

Visited Disneyland at age five but didn't like the crowds. Has a cat named Lancelot and a dog named Gila. Is the author of the acclaimed Bronze Hammer series, which won the coveted Tweedle Award for Young Adult Literature. First book was published at the age of 15. Currently lives in a castle in the mountains of Romania with her husband, Herbert, and their twin sons, Thor and Wulff. She collects medieval armor and weapons. Her collection is on loan to a museum in Topeka, Kansas. Her father was a coal miner in West Virginia until the age of 22, when he met his future wife, Patsy. They moved to British Columbia where he did forestry work. Samantha was born in Victoria, B.C. in 1978. When she was young she loved to read King Arthur stories and anything involving dragons. She collects dragons to this day and has over 2,000 in her collection. Samantha spends her free time mountain climbing, doing extreme mountain biking, photographing lizards, and writing poems about dragons (none of which are yet published). She would like to write a screenplay for *The Silver Sword*, provided someone purchases the film rights. In her own words, "I write the kinds of books I would love to have read when I was fourteen or fifteen. Teens make the best audience because their imaginations are limitless."

(226 words)

A Writer's Questions

Are there certain kinds of information that should not be included in a bio? Might some questions be inappropriate for an interview? How so?

Presentation Matters

Now it's your turn to write a bio from the ground up. That means you will have to choose the person you'd like to write about, do some research/interviews, and decide what goes in and what does not. You may choose to write about one of the following.

- An author whose work you admire
- Someone you know, famous or not (His or her book can be hypothetical!)

Plan to complete the following steps.

1. Collect information through research and/or interviews.

2. Include information suitable for a bio.

3. Include details that would interest readers.

4. Select a font and layout both eye-catching and appropriate for the featured person. (Photo or art may be included.)

5. Complete your final draft on the computer, if possible.

6. Limit your bio to 100 words. (It should fit the inside panel of a book jacket.)

NOTE: To add visuals, you can import non-copyrighted art from the Internet or borrow photos from a personal collection, provided you have permission to do so. Simpler yet, just insert a rough sketch, indicating the kind of photo or other artwork you would like to see.

Sample Paper 3

Score for Ideas _____

Sharks: Misunderstood Inhabitants of the Sea

There may be stranger looking creatures in the ocean, but none are more misunderstood than sharks. Whose fault is that? Ours. The Internet is filled with information on sharks, but most of us don't trouble to dig too deeply. Sharks usually make the news when a human is attacked, so we tend to think that swimmers who aren't attacked just got lucky. You won't see headlines that read "Sharks Ignore Divers." Much of what we believe about sharks is based on rumors, fear, and sensationalist news footage. Let's debunk a few myths.

The closest most humans come to sharks is when they see them in the movies or on the TV. Usually, these images feature a wild feeding frenzy, with dramatic close-ups of teeth, fins and thrashing tails. This makes for great video footage, but in real life, feeding frenzies are rare. Most sharks hunt and eat alone. Only when there is a large kill do other sharks move in.

Thanks to the 1975 film *Jaws*, people see a shark's dorsal fin and think of a 25-foot Great White whose sole mission in life is hunting down humans. You've probably got the music in your head now. The movie trailer presented the Great White as a mindless eating machine who would attack and devour anything. But remember, movie trailers are created to sell tickets, not educate us. The fact is, sharks are the ones who should be afraid. Look at the numbers: 100 million sharks die every year at the hands of humans, while 30 humans lose their lives to sharks. That's far fewer than the number of people killed by dogs, horses or lightning strikes.

Although no one wants to be attacked by a shark, it is simply not true that they are regularly on the hunt. (Turn off that music in your head.) In fact, sharks are downright lazy, and will often just hide along the bottom of the sea or behind a coral reef waiting for suitable prey.

They aren't waiting for humans, either—they much prefer fish. Most sharks are smaller than people and eat fish smaller than themselves. True enough, sharks can be excited by the smell of blood, and their sense of smell is close to 10,000 times sharper than that of humans. Going in the water with an injury or an open wound is probably one of the most dangerous things a diver or swimmer can do. It can also be dangerous to lie on a surfboard with your swim fins hanging off the edge. To the shark beneath you, you might look very much like a seal. One bite tells the shark it has made a mistake, but that's small comfort to the person who is bitten.

Learning the facts about sharks is the only way to fight the fear and misunderstanding most people have about these important sea creatures. Did you know that sharks don't have bones, that a group of sharks is called a *shiver,* that one species of shark is only seven inches long, that the presence of sharks helps keep the Great Barrier Reef ecosystem balanced? Knowing a few facts is a start, but find out more. Don't rely on the movies. Go to an aquarium and see sharks up close. Chances are, a marine biologist will treat you to a quick overview. Then, if you're daring, swim with the sharks. Hundreds of companies will take you out for an experience you will remember forever. You'll discover that sharks are graceful, curious—and cautious. And if you do swim with them, they may discover that humans aren't as bad as *they* heard.

Sources

Sharks and Other creatures of the deep. New York, NY: DK Publishing, 2008.

Cousteau, Jean-Michel. *Cousteau's Great White Shark.* Published in 1995 by Harry N. Abrams.

Hoyt, Erich. *Creatures of the Deep,* by Erich Hoyt. Published by **Firefly Books** in 2001.

Lee, B. "Save the Sharks." *Associated Content.* 22 Oct. 2009 <http://www.associatedcontent.com/article/549319/save_the_sharks_the_truth_a_misunderstood.htm?cat=47>.

Sample Paper 4

Score for Ideas _____

Stop Smoking Now!

Quitting smoking can be very hard. As everyone knows, smoking is an addiction. That means you can become addicted to smoking just like you can become addicted to drugs, alcohol, or gambling. There have been a lot of books written and movies made about how these kinds of addictions can ruin families, cause divorce, homelessness, and cause injury or death. These are very sad stories but can also be inspirational, too. People that have battled back against a life of drugs can help others fight their addictions.

If you grow up in a house where both parents smoke, you are more likely to become a smoker than if you lived in a house of nonsmokers. The same kind of thing is true for drugs and alcohol, too. If a person has a parent who is an alcoholic, alcoholism can be in their genes and it can be passed on to future generations. This may also be true of gambling, though more research on this is needed.

If you don't start smoking, it will save you lots of money and your food will taste better. You won't have to keep going outside at family gatherings or at work (if your company has a no smoking policy). Quit now to save your health and your money. Every day 3,000 young people decide to experiment with smoking. Don't be one of them! Don't let phony advertising trick you!

Sources

http://www.smoking-facts.net/Teen-Smoking-Facts.html

http://listverse.com/2009/01/11/30-fascinating-cigarette-smoking-facts/

http://www.winternet.com/~terrym/quitsmoke.html

Name _____   Date _____

Revising Checklist for Ideas

☐ I chose a writing topic I like and I'm excited about it. OR

☐ I want to change my topic to _____.

☐ I have all the information I need to make writing easy. OR

☐ I could get more information from _____.

☐ My main idea is focused and manageable. OR

☐ I'm going to shrink it down to this: _____.

☐ Details expand my discussion or story for readers. OR

☐ I need to include details that answer these readers' questions:

_____?

_____?

_____?

☐ I crossed out any filler (unneeded information that interrupts the main message). OR

☐ I didn't have any filler!

☐ My title hints at the main idea without telling *too* much.

☐ I shared my writing with _____.

That person's rating of my ideas:

| 1 | 2 | 3 | 4 | 5 | 6 |

Note Don't use this checklist just to compliment yourself, even if your writing is terrific! Use it to plan revisions or additions. Try to see your writing the way a reader who doesn't know you would see it.

Name _____ Date _____

Revising Checklist for Conventions and Presentation

☐ After writing my draft, I waited 3 days to edit so I could see it fresh.

☐ I read my writing twice to check for errors—once silently, once aloud.

☐ I looked carefully at these things:

    ☐ capitalization   ☐ spelling   ☐ grammar
    ☐ punctuation   ☐ paragraphing

☐ There are NO distracting errors (even tiny ones) to slow a reader down or get in the way of the message.

☐ I used punctuation to bring out meaning and voice.

☐ I used *italics* to show readers which words to *emphasize* in reading aloud.

☐ I used **boldface** to make important terms stand out.

☐ IF I used dialogue, I started a new paragraph for each new speaker, and

☐ I used quotation marks to mark each speaker's words.

☐ I designed my presentation to catch a reader's eye.

☐ My presentation makes the "informational trail" easy to follow.

☐ I made important information (facts, names, dates, definitions) easy to find.

☐ My presentation will make the message clear.

☐ I shared my writing with _____

That person's rating of my conventions and presentation:

1	2	3	4	5	6

Note Good conventions and presentation are a matter of courtesy. After all, *someone* edits every piece of writing that is read. The question is, will that someone be you? Or will you leave the editing task to your reader?

Organization

Imagine that you open your math textbook one day and discover that the first page is numbered 51, the second 297, the third 32 . . . what's going on here? Everything's out of order! You phone the publisher to protest. Their casual response? "Hey, it's all *in* there—you just have to look." Sounds a little like a nightmare, doesn't it? Just how important *is* order anyway? When readers need information in a hurry or when they want to make sense of the message, order is not just helpful. It's vital. Readers can't appreciate the big picture when they have to spend all of their energy piecing that picture together for themselves.

In this unit, you'll learn to organize your writing by

- putting ideas in a logical order.
- keeping the spotlight on your main message.
- using transitions to connect ideas clearly.
- taking organization one step at a time.

Name _____   Date _____

Sample Paper 5
Score for Organization _____

How to Shop

Next time you're at the mall or grocery store, take a moment to watch the people around you. You'll discover that most of them are random shoppers. They go to stores for entertainment and wind up buying anything that grabs their attention. You don't want to be one of them. Here are four easy things to remember that can help you protect that money you worked so hard for.

First, make a list, and (here's the important part) follow it! If you do not follow it, there is no point in making it. Don't leave it at home and don't ignore it. It's your guide to shopping well. If you see something you really want that isn't on your list, write it on the back. Go home and think about it. If you still want it a week later, put it on your NEW list.

Second, make a budget and stick to it. Whether you are shopping for food or holiday presents, follow your budget like it's the law. If you don't know how to make a budget, start by figuring out what you are spending now. Write down every single item, even small things like socks or gum, for a month. Total it. If the total scares you or goes over your income, see what you can cut. There is always something! Many people blow their budgets by using credit cards. If you don't have the money to pay for something now, what will you do when the credit card bill comes? If you *must* use a credit card, set a per-purchase limit of X dollars and never, ever go over.

Third, avoid buying things on impulse. Store managers count on you to do this, so think of it as a game. Walk right by that first display—you know the one. It's right inside the front door and it holds something the store manager thinks you can't resist. Show him or her you can. Walk right by. Don't even look aside! Stores also love to put last-minute

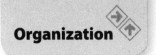

Name _____ Date _____

impulse purchases right by the cash register. You're waiting in line and during the delay (there's always a delay), you say to yourself, "Oh, it's only . . ." Fill in the blank: a soda, a pack of gum, a magazine. Last month, I bought a racing game. I don't use it, and now I wish I had the money back. I can't recover my money, but I got something better—a lesson in good shopping. Now, I take a deep breath and walk outside for a few minutes to give myself time to think. It's working. I haven't made a single impulse purchase since.

The last suggestion is probably the hardest. To be a good shopper, you have to know the difference between *wanting* something and *needing* something. My dad says it can take most of your life to figure this out. If you want something, you save up for it. That means waiting, which for most people sounds like suffering. Get over it. Here's the difference: I *need* shoes, but if I *want* the ones that cost $200, I have to wait until I've saved the money.

If you follow these four suggestions, something terrific happens. You don't have that feeling of guilt as you head home from the store—or the feeling of dread that goes with waiting for your credit card bill. With your list in your hand and your budget in your head, you can have a lot of fun watching other shoppers make the mistakes you used to make.

Name _____   Date _____

Sample Paper 6
Score for Organization _____

Shopping by Computer

Last week I bought a bunch of stuff online on my computer. It's really easy. Anyone can do it. My grandfather just got a new computer for his birthday, but he has not taken it out of the box. I don't know if he will ever hook it up. He also has difficulty driving, so if he did have the computer hooked up, he could do a lot of his shopping online. That way he would not have to drive in bad weather. My parents worry when he drives because he has a very hard time parking. And it is completely unnecessary. Of course, shopping online is not as fun as meeting your friends at the mall! Obviously!

You can buy groceries online from some grocery stores. Then you can go pick them up or have them delivered. Books are another thing you can buy online. My grandfather reads all the time, so this is one of the main things he would buy. You can also buy a plane ticket online. My mom and dad travel and they get good deals on their tickets. You can order just about anything, in fact, I can't think of anything you can't order by using a computer. There are shipping costs involved so be sure to check that out before you order. If you think about it, it is easier to sit down at the computer than to go to the mall. (For some people, anyway.) Besides, look at the gas you will save. Everything you want (and also some stuff you don't need, unfortunately) is just one click away. You could wind up buying a lot of things you do not really need, but you will really have fun once you learn a few secrets to shopping carefully.

Organization

The WRITER...
opens with an inviting lead.

So the READER...
_____
_____
_____

The WRITER...
organizes information to showcase the message.

So the READER...
_____
_____
_____

The WRITER...
uses helpful transitions.

So the READER...
_____
_____
_____

The WRITER...
closes with a satisfying conclusion.

So the READER...
_____
_____
_____

Organization's a Joke

Just kidding. But they do have something in common. Order and timing are everything when you're telling a joke. You have to set it up, tell enough so the joke makes sense, then end with a zinger. It doesn't work to put the punch line right up front and then say, "Oops! Pretend I didn't get to that part yet!" Good writing follows a similar sequence. It opens with a strong lead, expands the main idea in the middle, and ends with a zinger: the conclusion. There's an art to telling a joke well. And there's an art to sequencing information in writing.

Sharing an Example: *Moby Dick*

In his novel *Moby Dick*, Herman Melville tells the story of Captain Ahab's bloodthirsty obsession with killing the tremendous white whale. In the following passage, Ahab paces the quarter-deck as he eyes his men. As you read, notice how Melville *sequences* the dialogue, making his message clearer with every sentence.

Vehemently pausing, he cried— "What do ye do when ye see a whale, men?"

"Sing out for him!" was the impulsive rejoinder from a score of voices.

"Good!" cried Ahab, with a wild approval in his tones; observing the hearty animation into which his unexpected question had so magnetically thrown them.

"And what do ye next, men?"

"Lower away, and after him!"

"And what tune is it ye pull to, men?"

"A dead whale or a [sunken] boat!"

Moby Dick
by Herman Melville

Quick Reflection

Take a moment to think about the passage you just read. What is the big idea the author wants readers to take away from this passage?

_____

_____

_____

What If . . .

What if the author had been a little careless about sequence? Let's say he wrote in a hurry—or didn't go back to reread what he had written. In that case, his writing might have looked more like the following passage. This version has one sentence out of sequence—and it's missing another. *Without looking back*, underline the out-of-order sentence and draw an arrow to show where it should go. Insert a caret (∧) to show where a sentence is missing.

Vehemently pausing, he cried— "What do ye do when ye see a whale, men?"

"Good!" cried Ahab, with a wild approval in his tones; observing the hearty animation into which his unexpected question had so magnetically thrown them.

"And what do ye next, men?"

"Lower away, and after him!"

"A dead whale or a [sunken] boat!"

"And what tune is it ye pull to, men?"

Quick Reflection

How easy was it for you, as a reader, to notice when something was missing or out of place?

☐ It was VERY easy! The problems leaped right out at me!

☐ It was pretty easy—but I had to read the passage several times.

☐ It was impossible. In fact, the second version sounded just fine to me.

Playing with Order

This writer struggled with order—then finally gave up and cut his whole story apart into nine sentence strips. Read everything carefully—more than once. Then, with a partner (or in a writing circle), number the sentences in an order you think makes sense—and tells a good story. Remember the sequence of a well-timed joke: set-up, expansion, punch line.

_____ Strays often show up during winter when the ground is covered with snow and hunting gets tough.

_____ Honey Pie, as my grandma named her, now sleeps by the wood stove.

_____ I say lucky because my grandma has a soft spot in her heart for lonely strays—especially when the snow is two feet thick.

_____ Most of them are old or injured.

_____ This is not unusual.

_____ We always visit them during the holidays.

_____ Last year, about a week before our
visit, a stray calico took up
residence inside the horse barn.

_____ This particular stray was
no more than a kitten—a very
lucky one at that.

_____ My grandparents live on an 80-acre
farm just outside Spokane.

Taking One More Look

The two most important parts of a joke are the opening
line and the punch line. And as it turns out, beginnings and
endings are critical to most writing. Take another look at the
sentence you identified as the lead (#1) for the story about
the stray kitten. Write a stronger version here—one that will
really get your reader hooked:

_____

_____

_____

_____

Now, take another look at the sentence you identified as
the conclusion (#9). Write an even more satisfying version
here—one that leaves a lingering thought or image in the
reader's mind:

_____

_____

_____

_____

Name _____   Date _____

Share and Compare

When you've finished your revisions, read the whole story aloud, including your revisions, with a partner or in a writing circle. Does everything make sense? Assess your work using this list:

- ☐ I set up my story with a strong lead that will hook readers.

- ☐ I put every sentence into a sequence that makes sense.

- ☐ I ended with a conclusion that will leave readers thinking—or give them something to remember.

A Writer's Questions

In this lesson, you had all of the sentences needed to create a story. Could there be more than one right way to arrange them? How so? Do you think good writers look for various possible ways to sequence information?

Putting It to the Test

When you're taking a writing test, you won't have time to take sentences apart and play with the order—obviously! But is there a little planning trick you could use to help you put things in an order that's at least logical?

Avoid the Wandering Spotlight

The theater goes dark. The curtains open. The spotlight clicks on, illuminating an actor who is speaking the opening lines of a play. Suddenly, the spotlight jumps from the actor to an audience member in the front row, then to the ceiling, and then back to the now confused actor who continues to speak—forgetting a line or two. Imagine the people in the audience as they try to concentrate on the play. What will they remember most about this experience—the performance or the wandering spotlight?

When a writer takes the "spotlight" away from the main topic, readers have trouble following the story or conversation. Like the confused audience in the theater, they get distracted. Give your readers some guidance by keeping the spotlight focused on the main message.

Sharing an Example: "Night Sky"

Carefully read "Night Sky" aloud, quietly. Try to identify the writer's big idea and ask yourself, "Where is that spotlight focused? *Is* that spotlight focused?"

Night Sky

Ever since I can remember, my mother has told me about the constellations and their stories. Orion, Cassiopeia, Taurus, and Draco have always been my favorites. When I see them now, I don't just see the stars; I see the tragedy or the heroism behind

Organization

Name .... Date ....

these characters' lives. Heroes nowadays are a lot different. They're people you hear about on the news. There's so much violence that sometimes I don't like to even watch the news. I can keep up on the Internet, and that lets me choose the stories I want to hear, or even write in my own opinions. One of my favorite stargazing memories is when I was maybe three or four. It was really cold—I think it was January—so my mom and I both snuggled inside the same sleeping bag to keep warm. She pointed out the prominent three stars that make up Orion's belt. The three stars are also known as the Three Kings, the Magi, and the Arrow. Whenever I hear that name the Magi, I think of "The Gift of the Magi," a short story by O. Henry that we had to read for school. I wrote a paper about it, and if you haven't read it, you should. It is really good, and you will not guess the ending.

Reflection

As a <u>reader</u>, what are your thoughts about "Night Sky"?

☐ The writer kept the spotlight focused right on the main idea.

☐ The writer wandered once—but came right back.

☐ This writer's spotlight bounced around like a dizzy firefly!

Based on your reading, what do you think is the main idea of "Night Sky"? Share your thoughts here: _____

_____

_____

Share and Compare

Meet with a partner or in your writing circle to share your thoughts about "Night Sky." Does this writer have more than one main idea? Can she connect her ideas—and if so, how would she do that?

Refocusing

Read "Night Sky" again with a pen or pencil in hand. As you read, draw a line through parts you think are best left for another time. When you finish, read what is left to see if it is focused and makes sense. **HINT:** What you choose to cross out will depend on how you define the main message.

Share with a partner and assess your work:

☐ I didn't cut enough. That spotlight is still bouncing around.

☐ I cut a lot. Now the paper is mostly about constellations.

☐ I cut enough to create a new main idea.

Planning to Stay Focused

Focus doesn't just happen. It comes from
- having a clear main message.
- connecting all pieces within the writing to that message.

Here's your chance to plan your writing in a way that will keep the main message right in the spotlight. First, you need a topic. Take a "thinking minute" and see if you can recall a memory vivid enough to describe in one or two paragraphs. It could be
- a recent memory.
- something from your early childhood.

We've started an idea web for you on the next page to help you plan. Once you know which memory to write about, write a word or phrase that describes it right in the middle, inside the big circle. Then, fill in connected details—as fast as you can think of them—in the outer circles. Add more circles as you need them. You are the writer. Only YOU know how many details you need.

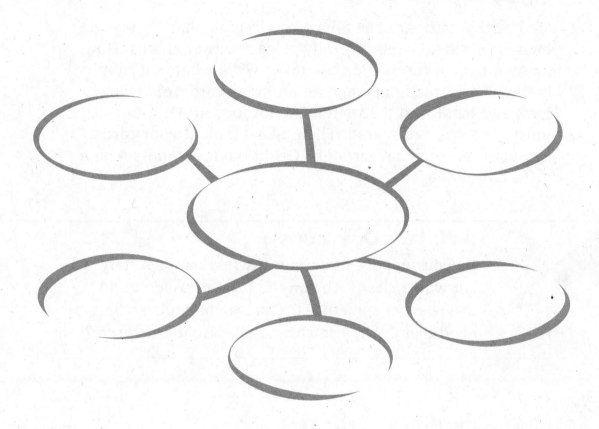

Creating a Focused Draft

How do you know when your web is done? Something in your head says, "I'm ready to write." And you begin to see your draft in your mind—like those constellation pictures in the sky. It might be

- a poem
- a memoir
- a description
- a character sketch

or something else. Write what you see in your mind—and keep going for 10 minutes or more, nonstop. Use your own paper.

Name   Date

Share and Compare

Meet with a partner or in a writing circle to share your
memory drafts. Listen carefully as each writer shares. How
many different forms did they take? Write what you think
is the writer's main message on an index card, fold it in
half, and hand it to the writer. Do not look at ANY cards
until everyone has shared. Then take a look at your cards.
Did your message get through? Or did your listeners hear a
different message?

A Writer's Questions

Do you suppose professional writers always start
out with a clear focus on the main message or do
they wander sometimes? Can wandering even be a
good thing? Why? How could you use it as a writer?

Putting It to the Test

When you're taking a writing test, sticking with a
main message is VERY important because you are
responding to someone else's prompt, not your
own. What are some good tips for not wandering
in this situation?

Staying Connected

If links in a chain aren't connected, they don't really form a chain. They're just a bunch of metal loops—no longer useful for towing a car, holding back a crowd, or keeping a wandering dog in its yard. The ideas in sentences and paragraphs also need to be clearly linked—connected, that is. Break the chain, and you force the reader to make his or her own connections—which may or may not be the ones you had in mind! In writing, connections are also called *transitions*. Writers use transitions to show readers how one idea or sentence relates to another, or how everything connects to a larger main idea. Strong transitions help sentences, paragraphs, and even chapters work together to create one smooth, coherent message.

Sharing an Example: *Leaving Home*

"Sooner or later, we all leave home." That's the lead (and part of the main message) in the book *Leaving Home* by Sneed B. Collard III. In the following two paragraphs, Mr. Collard describes how whales and Gila monsters leave the "comforts" of home. Follow these steps:

- Listen as your teacher or someone in your writing circle reads the passage aloud.
- Don't follow along with your *eyes*. Just hear the transitions in your mind.
- Read the passage on your own, silently. See if the transitions you heard are the ones we marked in **blue bold.**

Each winter, mother gray whales give birth to their calves in warm lagoons along the Pacific coast of Mexico. The calves nurse for several weeks. In spring, they accompany their mothers on a 7,000-mile journey to northern coastal feeding grounds. No one is sure how, but the whales know exactly where they are going and often show up at the same feeding grounds year after year. In the fall, the young whales find their way back to Mexico completely on their own.

Unlike whales, Gila monsters and most other animals are born without knowing exactly where they should go. But most animal babies do have instincts to guide them. Once they hatch or are born, their instincts may tell them to follow certain smells, seek out water, or find holes to live in. Many young animals make mistakes and die or are eaten, but the fortunate ones find the food, water, and shelter they need to survive.

Leaving Home
by Sneed B. Collard III

Words That Connect

On the next page is a list of transitions, transitional phrases, and linking words. They are grouped by purpose. Look over the list. Then consider adding it to your writing notebook. (As you run across other transitions in your reading, add them to the list.)

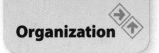

Name _____ Date _____

Transition Words

To show **location**

above	behind	by	near	outside
across	below	down	nearby	over
against	beneath	in back of	next to	throughout
along	beside	in front of	off	to the right
among	between	inside	onto	under
around	beyond	into	on top of	

To show **time**

about	continually	just then	now	today
after	during	lately	second	tomorrow
afterward	each time	later	soon	until
at	finally	meanwhile	suddenly	whenever
before	first	moments later	then	while
constantly	for a while	next	third	yesterday

To set up a **comparison**

also	as well	in the same way	likewise
as	equally	like	similarly

To set up a **contrast**

all the same	even so	nevertheless	otherwise	while
although	from another	nonetheless	still	yet
but	perspective	on the other	to see it	
	however	hand	another way	

To create **emphasis**

especially	in fact	to be sure	truly
for this reason	most important	to emphasize	

To **conclude** or **summarize**

after all	at length	finally	therefore
all in all	because	in conclusion	to sum up
as a result	conclusively	in the end	ultimately

To **add information** or **set up an example**

additionally	and	besides	furthermore	next
again	anyway	finally	in addition	other
along with	another	for example	in other words	what's more
also	as well as	for instance	moreover	

Name _____   Date _____

Hunting for Connections

Read the following passage and underline any transitions you find. Refer to the list of transition words to help you— but remember that not all transitions appear on that list.

As soon as I adopted Jake from the shelter, I knew I had to train him to do two things: curb the drooling and sit. Jake was a droopy-mouth kind of dog, however, so my first goal was hopeless. I decided to focus on the second.

Before we started sitting lessons, I had to hit the Web to figure out what to do. A food reward seemed like a safe bet, as well as plenty of time and patience.

The next day, I armed myself with doggie treats and took Jake out to our neighborhood park for his first lesson. It was a beautiful day for some dog training. I removed his leash, wiped the drool from my hand, and then pushed down on his rear end.

"Sit," I commanded. "Sit, boy."

Suddenly, Jake spotted a squirrel. He let out a hearty bark and took off running, with me crying out behind him.

An hour later, I was a sweating, exhausted mess. Jake had happily chased three squirrels, a Frisbee, and a flock of birds, but we were no closer to him actually sitting. In the end, I decided to skip the part where the treats were a reward and instead used them as a lure. In other words, I had to bribe my dog to sit.

Hey, don't laugh. It worked.

Share and Compare

Meet with a partner or in a writing circle to share the transitions you found in the passage about training a dog. Did you hear the same connections? Underline any transitions you might have missed. Then fill in your response.

Name _____ Date _____

The passage contains

☐ many, many transitions. Things are so well connected that it just flows.

☐ a few transitions, but it could use a lot more.

☐ almost NO transitions. I could barely make sense of it.

Making a Chain of Thought

Writing can have three kinds of transitional problems:

- **Transition overload,** in which the writer uses transitions even when they aren't needed
- **Missing transitions,** in which the writer forgets to connect ideas
- **Misuse,** in which the writer uses the *wrong* transition, leaving the reader confused

Read the following passage carefully, pencil in hand. Feel free to insert, delete, or replace transitions to create a smooth, logical chain of thought. **HINT:** Feel free to reword sentences as needed.

I'm not sure how it happened, so therefore, my room is a disaster! On the other hand, there are clothes, books, and games everywhere—including on the floor. At last, clean and dirty clothes are piled on chairs and across my bed. However, the space that is supposed to be my desk is too cluttered to work on. For one thing, my mom is wondering where the carpet went because she can't see any trace of it. My dad says to forget about the carpet. He worries where the awful smell is coming from. On the other hand, that smell has gotten so bad that I won't even have any friends come over. For example, I'm going to clean my room before I lose all contact with my friends, lose all my valuable stuff, or am grounded by my parents. Nevertheless, I could be cited for a fire hazard, and then, at long last, I will have more trouble!

Share and Compare

Meet with a partner or in a writing circle to share your revisions of the paper about the cluttered room. Talk about the kinds of revisions you did. Were you primarily taking transitions *out*—or putting new ones *in?* Is the chain of thought clear?

A Writer's Question

Choose any recent piece of writing from your writing folder. Read it carefully and lightly circle any transitional words or phrases you see. What did you find?

- ☐ I used *many* good transitions. I'm a transition champ!
- ☐ I didn't use too many transitions, but the chain of thought is clear anyway.
- ☐ I didn't use enough transitions. But now I know how to add them.

Putting It to the Test

Are certain kinds of transitions connected to certain genres of writing? Look back at the list of transition words. Are there particular transitional words or phrases that would be especially useful in a narrative piece? Informational essay? Persuasive essay? Why?

Putting the Puzzle Together

If you've ever put together a giant jigsaw puzzle, you know it's easier if you follow certain steps: turn *all* of the pieces right-side up, search for corner pieces and those flat-edged pieces that form the border, group pieces by color or other clues, and maybe sneak a peek at the picture on the box cover. (Yeah, some people think that's cheating.) As a writer, you already may have figured out that it helps to tackle organization step by step, too. After all, this trait is complex. In this lesson, you'll

- write a thesis sentence,
- select details to support it,
- create a strong lead,
- work on connecting ideas, and
- wrap up everything with a dynamite conclusion.

The result should be as clear as that picture on the puzzle box.

What's My Thesis?

Imagine you're writing a short chapter for a class book about amazing and dangerous sea creatures. You've gathered 20 details on your subject the stonefish. Now what?

One of the first organizational tasks any writer faces is deciding which pieces of information to keep and which ones to toss. You can't really make this decision until you have a thesis. So begin with that. Look through the list of

details. Do some go together to support a main message?
Use those to create a one-sentence thesis. Write it here:

Topic: Stonefish

Thesis: _____

_____

☐ **1.** Stingrays only sting when they are stepped on.

☐ **2.** Stonefish look like rocks but with venomous spines along
their back.

☐ **3.** Stonefish are camouflaged by their green to brown mottled
coloration.

☐ **4.** The spines of stonefish are sharp and strong enough to
pierce a shoe.

☐ **5.** Jellyfish have tentacles with millions of stinging cells.

☐ **6.** A Portuguese man-of-war is not a true jellyfish.

☐ **7.** Stonefish are the most venomous fish known to live in
the ocean.

☐ **8.** Stonefish habitats are usually around coral reefs, near
rocks, or on the muddy sea bottom.

☐ **9.** Stonefish live in the ocean.

☐ **10.** Stonefish may grow up to 12 inches long.

☐ **11.** Stonefish eat mainly shrimp, crustaceans, and small fish.

☐ **12.** The sting from a stonefish will swell rapidly and cause
extreme pain.

☐ **13.** The scorpionfish is also venomous.

☐ **14.** Stonefish are one of many poisonous, dangerous creatures
you will find in Australia.

☐ **15.** They are also known as reef stonefish.

☐ **16.** The stonefish has 13 spines along its back and each spine has two venom sacs.

☐ **17.** Stonefish are sometimes sold for their meat.

☐ **18.** The venom of a stonefish can kill humans if not treated.

☐ **19.** It may help weaken the venom and ease pain if a hot compress is applied or the wound is submerged in hot water.

☐ **20.** The pain from a stonefish sting can be so painful that victims ask to have the limb amputated.

Keep It or Toss It?

Read through the list of details again, carefully. Check (√) each piece of information you will keep because it supports your thesis. Omit anything that

- doesn't fit,
- is too general,
- isn't interesting enough, or
- is common knowledge.

Add to the List

Searching online or using any resources available, look for a few additional pieces of information that will add to your thesis. Write them here:

1. _____

2. _____

3. _____

Talk about your final list of details with your partner or in your writing circle. Do you have:

☐ Enough details

☐ Strong, intriguing, unusual details

☐ Too many details

Adjust your list any way you need to.

Grab the Reader's Attention . . .

Here's a lead sentence you could use:

This will be a report about the venomous stonefish.

Please don't. You really need to grab your reader's attention with the first sentence, and an announcement won't do it. Look over your list of "keeper" details—and your new details. Does anything stand out as startling, interesting, or even odd? Begin with that. Write your lead (a sentence or two) here:

_____

_____

_____

_____

_____

_____

. . . and Keep Ideas Flowing!

Already you've

- narrowed your list of details and
- written a striking lead.

Look at your details one more time to get them in your head. Then write. Use your own paper and keep your pencil moving for at least 10 minutes. Glance at your detail list from time to time to keep ideas flowing in your head. **HINT:** You do NOT have to use every single detail. Good writers never do.

Sharing Your Efforts

Just how complete is your puzzle? Let's find out. With your partner, take turns reading your stonefish paragraphs. Listen carefully for what's strong, and help each other figure out what the next step should be. Use this list to help you.

- ☐ Strong lead
- ☐ Easy-to-follow sequence
- ☐ Spotlight on the main idea
- ☐ Smooth transitions that link ideas or sentences
- ☐ Powerful conclusion that wraps things up

A Writer's Questions

Maybe you're not thinking of publishing the stonefish piece you wrote for this lesson. But what if you were? What's the very next thing you would work on? What about after that? Do you have a clear vision of the steps involved in organizing information effectively?

Putting It to the Test

We've seen how important leads and conclusions are in any piece of writing. Can you think of some standard leads or conclusions a writer would be wise to avoid when writing an on-demand essay? Remember, readers who score thousands and thousands of essays have heard some leads and conclusions—well, let's just say, *many* times.

Paragraphs: The Building Blocks of Writing

Writers are skilled at turning small blocks of meaning into bigger blocks. Words form sentences, and sentences form paragraphs (which then form chapters, then books, and sometimes whole series).

Paragraphs are especially important because they chunk information—the way files in a cabinet keep letters in one section and articles in another. Without paragraphs, readers couldn't just open a book and dive in. They would have to start by figuring out what went with what. As a writer of logical paragraphs, you can spare your readers all that trouble.

A Warm-Up

Look through any book from your classroom—novel, nonfiction, anything with paragraphs. Choose one paragraph with at least five sentences. Read it aloud to yourself. Think about the way it's put together: the way it begins, how the information flows from one sentence to the next, the way it ends—or makes a connection to the upcoming paragraph. Use this space to write down your thoughts. You don't need to write whole sentences. Just make quick notes.

_____

_____

_____

_____

_____

Now use what you know to make a paragraph out of the following five sentences. Number them in an order that makes sense. It is fine to work with a partner.

_____ If you have, then you know that Coyote spends each cartoon trying to capture the Road Runner.

_____ Road Runner always outsmarts Coyote in the end and runs away.

_____ Beep-beep!

_____ Have you ever seen a Road Runner and Coyote cartoon?

_____ He invents or sends away for all sorts of exotic machines and methods to catch Road Runner, but they never work.

Share and Compare

Compare your paragraph with a partner's. Did you each put the sentences in the same order? Is there only one way to order these sentences? What is the test that any good sentence order needs to pass?

12 Sentences = X Paragraphs

Following are 12 sentences about vultures. Use them to form one or more paragraphs. Work with a partner or in a writing circle. **HINT:** Read aloud carefully—more than once—as you work.

Vultures

_____ As natural garbage disposals, vultures help keep many of these diseases from spreading to other animals and even humans.

_____ They are not bashful eaters, either.

_____ Unless you are a vulture, do not try this at home.

_____ Vultures have a few other strange behaviors and abilities to go along with their interesting food preferences.

_____ It's probably also fortunate that vultures don't have a great sense of smell.

_____ Vultures are nature's scavengers and clean the environment by eating dead animals.

_____ Luckily, considering their diet, vultures are naturally equipped with acids in their digestive systems able to eliminate disease bacteria like anthrax and cholera.

_____ But they do have amazing eyesight.

_____ It may sound gross, but they are able to eat and process animal carcasses in any condition, including diseased, rotting, or badly decayed.

_____ In fact, a flying vulture can spot a three-foot dead animal from four miles away!

_____ If a vulture needs to cool or even disinfect itself after feeding on rotten flesh, it urinates on its legs.

_____ Vultures have been known to eat up to 20 percent of their own body weight during one feeding.

Share and Compare

Compare your chunking of the 12 vulture sentences with the organizational structure another team came up with. Take turns reading aloud. Did you

- come up with the same number of paragraphs?
- chunk sentences the same way?
- order information in a way that makes sense?

What do you think? Is there a right answer to our equation:

12 sentences = X paragraphs

A Writer's Questions

Since all of the sentences in the preceding passage were about vultures, why not just put them all into one paragraph? Isn't that what a paragraph is—a group of sentences all on the same big topic? Or is there more to the definition?

Information on the Level

How do you usually read a book? Do you start with the very first word and read every single thing right through to the last word?   YES   NO

We want you to *really respond* to that question because it's important to this lesson. And if by chance you said yes, you are by no means alone. But it may surprise you to discover that a lot of very good readers do not read that way at all.

Some begin by looking at the table of contents, checking out chapter titles, or rapidly paging through the entire book to get a sense of the "territory"—how big it is, how many subtopics it covers, whether or not it has illustrations, and so on. Some readers never do get around to reading every single word—if (and here's the big *if*) they can find the information they need some other way.

Many writers design nonfiction books to accommodate these different reading styles, creating informational trails to allow reading on different levels:

- the **Big Idea** level (big print, main ideas, or facts of extreme interest)
- the **Graphic** level (photos, drawings, charts, or other illustrations)
- the **In-depth** level (smaller print, detailed information, more resources)

Font size, color, bold or italic print, and illustrations provide visual clues that direct a reader's eye to the level that's right for their informational needs.

A Warm-Up

Your teacher will show you one or more books illustrating the kinds of informational levels described here. (If you know of others, by all means mention them!) Look closely at these examples and see if you can follow the informational "trail" from page to page.

Try following just one trail. Ask yourself what kind of information it provides. Then answer this question: Which trail would you most likely follow if you were

- needing thorough research for a report?
- investigating a topic to see whether or not you wanted to learn more?
- considering purchasing a book for a friend who liked the topic?

Presentation Practice

Presenting the Levels

Look carefully at the following page advertising various types of cell phones. ("How it looks" is one of the deciding factors for cell phone buyers.) As a reader, can you find three different informational levels? How does the presentation style direct readers to each level?

Flip, Slide, Touch, PDA, Hybrid: Cell Phone Basics

The basic style, shape, and size can affect *every* aspect of cell phone use. Are you all about looking cool—or do you want a phone that fits your hand just right and will be easily retrievable from a pocket? We want to help you choose the phone that's right for you!

Type	Pros	Cons
Flip	Compact, protected screen, keyboard	Cover can break if dropped
Slide	Compact, opens to multiple keyboards	Awkward phone features
Touch	Varied LCD display of controls	Short battery life
PDA	Full qwerty keyboard	Heavier, power drain
Hybrid	Good for gaming, high cool factor	Cool features—more can go wrong

Meet with a partner or in a writing circle to discuss the cell phone advertisement. What do you like about it? Is anything missing? Together, respond to the following questions:

1. How easy was it to spot the three informational levels in the ad?

2. Which informational level did your eye go to first? Why?

3. Obviously, an ad cannot teach all there is to know about cell phones. But would this ad get a potential buyer ready to ask intelligent questions?

4. If you were in charge of designing this ad, what—if anything—would you change?

A Writer's Questions
Given the choice, will many readers follow ALL of the informational paths open to them? Why is that? Knowing—as you do now—that some nonfiction books contain multiple informational levels, do you think your style of reading might be a little different in the future? How so?

Presentation Matters

For this part of the lesson, meet with a partner or in a writing circle. Together, you will create a multi-page (three to five pages) picture book for younger readers on a topic of your choice. The book should be nonfiction, but it can be humorous and light. And as you know, picture books can cover sophisticated topics, so long as you use words that make complex concepts understandable to young readers.

Follow these steps:

1. Work together to choose a topic that is especially interesting to your group. Narrow it down to a manageable size— something you can explore well in three to five book pages. (Remember, for young readers, the amount of print per page will be less than for your own age group.)

2. Research your topic online or using books in your classroom or media center. Find the details you need to create an informational trail on three levels:
   - the **Big Idea** level (big print, main ideas, or facts of extreme interest)
   - the **Graphic** level (photos, drawings, charts, or other illustrations)
   - the **In-depth** level (smaller print, detailed information, more resources)

3. You may wish to divide the work by levels, so that each writer/designer has a specific task. You will also need someone to take on the job of layout—designing each page as a whole. Here's a summary of the tasks:

- The **Big Idea** level person identifies the main ideas to be emphasized on each page—and presents each one in a sentence or two, using big print.

- The **Graphic** level person chooses and designs visuals for each page, working closely with writers so visuals capture relevant details. Visuals may include maps, labeled drawings, and so on, in addition to sketches or photos.

- The **In-Depth** level person expands on the big ideas with detailed sentences written in smaller print.

- The **Layout** person works with the whole team to position items on each page. This person must consider fonts, colors, placement, and white space.

4. When you finish, share or display your results according to your teacher's instructions.

Name _____ Date _____

Sample Paper 7
Score for Organization _____

Going Organic

If it's organic, it's better for you. At least, that is what many people believe. The definition of organic talks about how the food is grown without using nasty chemicals or pesticides, and the packaging follows the same rules. It just makes sense. Science or common sense. You decide. Either way, it's a good argument. A lot of farmers are trying to get their farms certified as organic because the demand is growing. Not everyone eats organic food, however. Farmers must do many things before they can be certified, though.

In a lot of communities, farmers' markets (during part of the year) let people buy directly from the growers. Moreover, this saves a lot of fuel because food doesn't have to be shipped from across the country or world to get to you. For another thing, you can buy organic meats, vegetables, tea, wine, spices, milk, and even honey. Farmers' markets weren't that popular a few years ago.

When your food does not contain chemicals you are less likely to get certain kinds of cancers. Many people also say it just tastes better and fresher. It costs a lot more to produce organic food, so many people are growing their own organic food. This is not easy to do. You can buy books that show you how.

In conclusion, is organic food really more healthy? That is a big question.

Sources

Meyerowitz, Steve. *Organic Food: How to Shop Smarter and Eat Healthier*. Guilford, CT: Global Pequot Press, 2004.

To Everything There Is a Season. By: Hemmelgarn, Melinda, Current Health 2, 0163156X, Sep2008, Vol. 35, Issue 1

What is organic food? By: Mather, Mort, Mother Earth News, 00271535, Sep98, Issue 169

Is Organic Food Really Better for You? By: Sayre, Laura, Mother Earth News, 00271535, Dec2007/Jan2008, Issue 225

Sample Paper 8

Score for Organization _____

The California King

The California king snake, or Cal king, is one of the most interesting creatures in North America. Don't let the California part of its name fool you. This guy has little in common with tan, blond, surfer-dudes that hang out on the beach. In the wild, the Cal king is one very tough customer.

Birds, rodents, lizards, frogs, and other snakes better be on the alert when Cal king is on the hunt. It is one of the few creatures, including humans, that will approach a rattlesnake—and even stalk it. In fact, king snakes hunt and eat rattlesnakes, even though the rattlers are often larger. Although Cal kings are not immune to a rattler's venom, their systems are relatively tolerant of the poison, and it almost never kills them. The Cal kings themselves have no venom. Instead of relying on poison, they wrap themselves around their prey and squeeze! Then they unhinge their jaws to swallow the victim. They have other survival tricks going for them, too.

The California king snake bears a stunning resemblance to the deadly coral snake. People often confuse the two, sometimes with painful or even deadly results. What is more important for the king snake, though, is that its enemies, including hawks and eagles, also confuse the two snakes. The Cal king avoids numerous confrontations with predators thanks to mistaken identity—the predator may confuse the king snake with a coral snake and stay away. Looks can be important if you are trying to avoid attack.

Despite its reputation as a relentless hunter, the California king snake is gentle around humans, especially if they show no fear and make no sudden moves. They can make good pets, but you have to do your homework and learn about their habits and preferences. What do you think? Would you want one for a pet? Would you dare pick one up for a closer look? It's most likely a Cal king, but then again . . .

Sources

Applegate, Robert. **Kingsnakes & Milksnakes in Captivity.** 2007. ECO/Serpent's Tale NHBD.

Milksnakes and Tricolored Kingsnakes by Bartlett, Richard, and Patricia Bartlett, Barron's Educational Series, Hauppauge, NY. Published in 2000.

<http://lllreptile.com/info/library/animal-care-sheets/snakes/-/california-king-snake/>

<http://www.whozoo.org/Intro2000/vansibor/VanSib_CaliforniaKingsnake.htm>

Name _____ Date _____

Revising Checklist for Organization

☐ My lead sets the stage and gets your attention! OR . . .

☐ I should begin with: _____.

☐ My ending wraps things up and leaves you thinking. OR . . .

☐ I should end with: _____.

☐ This writing is easy for reader to follow. They will NEVER feel lost.

☐ I stayed with ONE main message or story, beginning to end.

☐ I have a surprise or two—not everything is completely predictable.

☐ Details and events seem to come at just the right moment.

☐ I would describe my overall design this way . . .

    ☐ Main idea and details or support

    ☐ Chronological events

    ☐ Comparison-contrast

    ☐ Problem-solution

    ☐ Series of questions with answers

    ☐ Visual description from first impressions to subtle details

    ☐ Other _____

☐ I used paragraphs to show small shifts in the story or discussion.

☐ I shared my writing with _____

That person's rating of my organization:

1	2	3	4	5	6

Note Good organization guides your reader through your writing as if you were shining a light on a dark path in the forest. Did you shine a light on the trail of your thinking—or leave readers in the dark?

Voice

Voice is often described as the writer's presence on the page. It's a spillover of the writer's own energy or enthusiasm, that special quality that touches readers' hearts and ignites their imaginations. Voice is distinctive and individual. It tells us who is speaking: Maya Angelou, Sharon Creech, Gary Paulsen, Jane Yolen—or *you*. We know that readers sometimes read purely for information. That's why they read the dictionary or a technical report. But often, they read for the sheer joy of it. Sheer joy comes from voice. Think of the books you love most and remember longest. Chances are, every one of them has voice.

In this unit you'll expand your understanding of Voice by

- creating a personal definition of voice.

- matching voice with purpose.

- using knowledge to create a confident informational voice.

- adjusting voice to reach a particular reader.

Sample Paper 9

Score for Voice _____

A Close Call

About a week ago, I saw a red-tailed hawk going after a Douglas squirrel. The squirrel was climbing a hundred-foot pine tree. The hawk flew at it, hoping for a quick kill, but the squirrel circled the tree to get out of the way. The hawk kept after the squirrel. Each time the hawk got close, the squirrel would go around to the other side of the tree. Finally the hawk gave up. It's probably difficult for hawks to fly too close to trees because of all the branches. The squirrel stayed in the tree for a while after the hawk left. I did not see where the hawk went. It did not come back. The squirrel did not come back either.

Sample Paper 10

Score for Voice _____

Toughest Thing on Two Legs

My grandmother likes to brag that she is the toughest thing on two legs. You're probably thinking that's a strange thing for an older lady to say. What's even stranger is that no one but my granddad ever challenges her. They don't dare. There's something about the look in her steely gray eyes that could scare a rattlesnake back into his hole.

Well, last summer my granddad had a chance to show Grandma that he was the toughest thing on two legs, but he didn't quite pull it off. He was cleaning out an old woodshed on his ranch, getting ready to tear it down because the wood was rotten. Even though Grandma had warned him plenty of times that old buildings make good hangouts for scorpions, Granddad insisted on going out there. Before long, we heard a yell from the shed, followed by a lot of words I won't repeat. I've heard my granddad get angry plenty of times, but this was above and beyond anything I'd ever heard before.

Grandma set down her coffee mug in time to see Granddad hobbling around the side of the shed, coming at a pretty good pace, biting his lip so he wouldn't let out another yell. She met him at the door, whipped off his shirt to make sure no other scorpions were hiding in it, pushed him into a chair, wrapped his hand in a cold, wet cloth, pumped two aspirins into him, and poured him a cup of coffee with cream, all in about one minute. Then she grabbed a hatchet and headed for the shed. Naturally, I followed, not wanting to miss anything. Something about an old lady with a hatchet kind of grabs your attention.

Name _____   Date _____

It took her only seconds, lifting boards with her toe (she had her boot on to protect her) to find the offending scorpion and dispatch it. She brought the body parts back to show Granddad—especially the scorpion's tail, where the stinger is. "Hardly big enough to make a person yell," she told Granddad, swinging the curly tail right in front of his nose. "But what really puzzles me is why you're limping when you got stung on the hand."

He didn't have an answer to that one, and I had to bite the insides of my cheeks to keep from laughing, though I was glad I wasn't the one who had been stung. I know who the toughest thing on two legs is, all right, but I also know enough to keep it to myself. That makes me the *smartest* thing on two legs.

Voice

The WRITER...
gets deeply involved with
the topic.

So the READER...

_____
_____
_____

The WRITER...
speaks in a natural, individual
voice.

So the READER...

_____
_____
_____

The WRITER...
speaks with confidence.

So the READER...

_____
_____
_____

The WRITER...
thinks about the reader
while writing.

So the READER...

_____
_____
_____

Creating a Personal Definition

One of the best ways to define voice is by reading. Each writer's voice is a little different, and some are so distinctive that we can recognize them even without being told who wrote the passage. (You might be such a writer yourself, now or in the future.) You'll hear voice described as energy, enthusiasm, individuality, personality, and confidence. These are all important elements of this complex trait. But in the end, the definition that should matter most to you is your own. This lesson is all about setting rubrics and checklists aside for a moment and defining voice in your own words, as you hear it. After all, it's that personal definition that will drive your own writing.

Who *Are* You?

Defining voice begins with figuring out who is behind the words. Sometimes we almost feel as if the writer is in the room with us, while other times we have no clear idea at all who is speaking. Carefully read each of the following passages, more than once, putting a "V" (for Voice) in the right margin each time you "hear" the writer's voice loud and clear. Try to picture each writer in your mind, and think of one or two words that describe that writer's voice.

Name _____ Date _____

Voice 1

Last weekend I went to a birthday party for my friend Becky. It was a skating party with lots of people. I was nervous about falling down, but I decided to be brave and just roll with it!

At the party, I fell down in front of everybody. Becky rolled over to see if I was OK. Everyone was staring at me. It was the most attention I had gotten all year! I decided to make the best of it. I stood up and took a moment to catch my balance. (OK, it took me more than a moment to catch my balance.) Then I gave a dramatic bow. Everyone laughed!

Words that describe the voice:

_____

_____

Voice 2

We went to bed with rain, and this morning when the alarm rang, there was more rain, coming down hard, smacking the windows. As much as I love fishing, waking up in the dark to the sound of a storm just makes me want to roll over. My feet protested as they hit the cold floor.

Our plan was to drive to the coast to catch the incoming tide on the Little Tillamook (our favorite river). Dad would paddle the canoe, and I would finally get to try out my fishing pole—the one I got weeks ago. I was a little worried. All this rain could muddy the water, making fishing next to impossible. We stopped for hot chocolate, and warmed our hands on the cups. The windshield wipers slapped back and forth in time to some lame 70s song. Dad was humming along like mad. I smiled in spite of the crummy weather, remembering that this day was about more than fishing.

Words that describe the voice:

_____

_____

Voice 3

   We headed out today to race at the school track. It is just for practice. We figured it would be a good warm-up for the track and field tryouts coming up next week. The person practicing with me is a fast runner and usually beats me. It will probably be the same thing today. We have been competitors for a while. I will do my best, but I doubt I'll win. Who knows, though.

Words that describe the voice:

_____

_____

Reflection

Think about the voices in the passages you read and talk about them with a partner or in a writing circle. Compare the words you used to describe each voice. Compare the writers you saw in your mind. Is each writer male or female? How old? Which voice would most likely keep you reading?

Rate each of the three voices on a scale of 1 (There's no human presence in this writing.) to 10 (Strong voice—I almost *know* this person!).

Voice 1 (the skating party)

Voice 2 (fishing in the rain)

Voice 3 (racing at the track)

Giving Voice a Boost

Look at the example you rated the *lowest* in the trait of Voice. Take a moment to read it again aloud. Think about what's missing and what you'd like to see or hear as a reader. Within your writing circle, make a plan to boost the voice of this piece. You might do any of the following.

- Change wording
- Add detail
- Write from a different point of view
- Write in two voices
- Write it as a poem or drama
- Or do anything else that occurs to you!

Write individually or create one group draft. Be prepared to share what you write aloud with the class.

Name _____ Date _____

Share and Listen

Take turns reading your revisions aloud. As you listen, be thinking about how you might define voice in your own mind. If you wish, make some notes here:

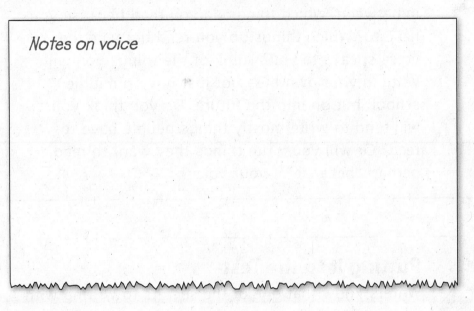

Notes on voice

Creating a Personal Definition

Think of the voices you heard throughout this lesson, the voices you love from your own reading, and the strategies you and others used to add voice to a short piece of writing. Then, write your own personal definition of voice here:

Voice is . . .

Name _____ Date _____

A Writer's Questions

Think of all the reading you do in your daily life, from grocery lists to novels and everything in-between. Which things do you read because you have to? Which things do you read because the voice speaks to you? Think of the things you will write in your own life—not just now in middle school, but on into the future. Do you think you will tend to write mostly things people have to read? Or will you write things they want to read, perhaps because of your voice?

Putting It to the Test

Writers know that one of the secrets to writing with strong voice is choosing a topic you care about personally and letting your strong feelings show. In a writing assessment, the topic is often chosen for you. If it's a topic you do not care for particularly, how can you, as a writer, overcome this barrier to strong voice?

Linking Voice to Purpose

Writing a set of directions for building a custom bicycle is different from writing a scary mystery story. Directions call for a helpful, experienced voice to help readers feel confident as they move carefully and purposefully from step to step. A good mystery calls for a voice that keeps readers engaged, curious, and on the edge of their seats as they rip through pages, biting their nails. As you will see in this lesson, voice often gives the reader some strong clues about a writer's purpose—to entertain, teach, persuade, update readers on the news, share a secret, give readers the shivers, and so on. Purposes for writing are endless, and so are the voices that go with them.

Sharing an Example: *Narrative of the Life of Frederick Douglass*

Here's a short example from Frederick Douglass's autobiography of how he threw off the bonds of slavery. Here, Douglass is unused to the harsh work he's forced to do. When he collapses, he draws the attention of the slave owner Mr. Covey. As you think about Douglass's account, ask yourself, "How would I describe this voice? And what is the writer's purpose?"

He came to the spot, and, after looking at me awhile, asked me what was the matter. I told him as well as I could, for I scarce had strength to speak. He then gave me a savage kick in the side, and told me to get up. I tried to do so, but fell back in the attempt. He gave me another kick, and again told me to rise. I again tried, and succeeded in gaining my feet; but, stooping to get the tub with

which I was feeding the [wheat] fan, I again staggered and fell.
While down in this situation, Mr. Covey took up the hickory
slat. . . and with it gave me a heavy blow upon the head, making a
large wound, and the blood ran freely; and with this again told me
to get up. I made no effort to comply, having now made up my mind
to let him do his worst.

Narrative of the Life of Frederick Douglass
by Frederick Douglass

Voice and Purpose

How would you describe the voice of Frederick Douglass?
Circle any word that applies. It's fine to circle more than
one or add your own words to our list.

nervous	inexperienced	angry	excited	confident
respectful	sad	curious	bored	terrified

Based on this voice, what do you think is the writer's
purpose? Check all that are true, and add your own
ideas also.

☐ To make us nervous and tense
☐ To paint a vivid picture in our minds
☐ To show how some slaves were treated
☐ To give us factual information about 19th century life
☐ To reveal what Mr. Covey is like
☐ To make us curious about American history
☐ To make us laugh
☐ To make us feel sorry for Frederick Douglass
☐ To make us wish we'd lived in the 1800s

My own ideas:

_____

_____

Name

Date

Different Voice—Different Purpose(s)

Here's a voice that's completely different. Again, listen carefully, thinking of words or phrases that might describe this author's voice. Also see if you can link the writer's voice to the purpose. (There may be more than one.)

There was a feller here once by the name of *Jim* Smiley, in the winter of '49—or maybe it was the spring of '50—I don't recollect exactly, somehow...but anyway, he was the curiousest man about always betting on anything that turned up you ever see, if he could get anybody to bet on the other side; and if he couldn't, he'd change sides... But still he was lucky, uncommon lucky; he most always come out winner. He was always ready and laying for a chance; there couldn't be no solit'ry thing mentioned but that feller'd offer to bet on it and take any side you please, as I was just telling you. If there was a horse race, you'd find him flush, or you'd find him busted at the end of it; if there was a dogfight, he'd bet on it; if there was a catfight, he'd bet on it; why, if there was a chicken fight, he'd bet on it; why, if there was two birds setting on a fence, he would bet you which one would fly first.

"The Celebrated Jumping Frog of Calaveras County"
by Mark Twain

Given the voice he uses, what is Mark Twain's purpose in writing this piece? List all the possible purposes you can think of—big or small.

1. _____

2. _____

3. _____

4. _____

5. _____

Voice

A Good Match?

Following is a news story about an electrical power blackout. A TV journalist will read this story to viewers. So, what's the primary purpose? And given that purpose, is this the right voice?

HINT: Pretend you're on TV as you read.

What a Blackout!

Wow! That was some blackout we experienced here in Woodville last night, wasn't it? Were you in town? If you were, you might have noticed (unless you were asleep or something! Ha, ha!) that the whole east side of the city from First Avenue up to Biloxi Boulevard was dark, dark, dark! We're talking no lights, no TV, no microwave, no power! One fallen tree and kapow! It was totally inconvenient—and even kind of creepy! Even the streetlights were out. The whole thing lasted for three hours, but it felt like days as people stumbled around in the dark. Probably some stubbed toes and bruised heads out there from bumping into things. Whoa! That's a blackout for you!

Does the voice match the purpose?

☐ It's a *perfect* match! This is how news sounds—and should sound.

☐ It needs a little tweaking, but the writer is on the right track.

☐ This is a total disconnect. The whole thing needs to be rewritten.

Name _____ Date _____

Emergency in the Newsroom!

Imagine you write for the news station. (Maybe you will one day!) The anchorperson who's supposed to read the news story about the blackout is in a panic. She says it doesn't sound right for viewers, and she can't do it. Luckily, you're on the job today! With your writing circle, make a plan.

1. Describe the kind of voice you think would be right for a report like this.

2. Look back at the draft. Underline words or phrases that are just wrong.

3. Revise by taking words out, rewriting, or adding any details you wish. It's OK to invent.

4. Read the final copy aloud. You MUST be able to read it within thirty seconds or less.

NOTE: Revise right on the copy. You do not need to rewrite unless you want to.

Share and Compare

Take turns reading your revised news stories aloud. Did every group find a voice to suit the purpose? Discuss the kinds of changes you made. And seriously, if a well-known TV journalist did use the original script, how would you feel about that? What would you think of the news station?

Voice

Name _____   Date _____

A Writer's Questions

What's the last time you can recall hearing or reading a voice that wasn't quite right for the purpose? Can you think of an example in books, on the Internet, on television or radio, or in real life? What was the effect on you?

Putting It to the Test

In on-demand writing, the purpose of the task is usually defined for you. It's built right into the prompt. As a writer, what would be your purpose as you responded to each of these prompts?

- Tell about a time when you were surprised.

- Many inventions have influenced our society. Explain how one invention has changed modern life.

- Some school rules seem unfair. Write a letter to your principal asking for one rule to be changed.

What sort of voice do you think matches each prompt? Look at some other examples of prompts online. See if the prompt alone gives you any clues about the purpose and voice readers might expect.

The Voice of Confidence

Expository or informational writing is intended to explore a topic or inform the reader. Uh-oh. That means a dry, droning voice, right? On the contrary. When you write a report for social studies or science, or when you analyze a piece of literature, you want your reader to feel the excitement that comes from learning something new. Of course, two things have to be true before you can share that kind of voice. First, YOU have to be excited. If you find your own topic hopelessly dull, it will be hard to drag others into a tedious conversation. Second, you need to know your stuff, whether through personal experience or research. That way, you can pick out extraordinary information to share, things readers haven't heard before. Knowing what you're talking about gives you confidence and that inspires trust. Once you gain their trust, readers tend to believe what you say. No wonder voice matters.

Sharing an Example: *G is for Googol*

An enthusiastic voice keeps readers engaged, and engaged readers learn and remember. In *G is for Googol: A Math Alphabet Book,* author David M. Schwartz uses a familiar format, an alphabet book, to explain some big math concepts. Read this passage about rhombicosidodecahedrons. Is this the confident voice of an expert? Or is this writer wishing he could write about something else?

"Excuse me?"

Rhombicosidodecahedron. (ROM-bi-cosi-DOE-DECK-a-HEE-dron.) Say it a few times, and it'll roll right off your tongue. You can impress your parents and your friends. You can say things like "Do you happen to have a rhombicosidodecahedron I can borrow?"

Now that you can pronounce it, perhaps you'd like to know what it is. A rhombicosidodecahedron is a special kind of *polyhedron.*

"What kind of polyhedron?" you say. "And what's a polyhedron, anyway?"

G is for Googol: A Math Alphabet Book
by David M. Schwartz

Reflection

Which of the following comes closest to matching your response to the passage from *G is for Googol?*

☐ Thank goodness it's over. I couldn't have taken one more line.

☐ Even though math isn't my favorite subject, this actually held my attention.

☐ It was terrific! If only other textbooks were written in this voice!

Searching for the Voice of Confidence

When you encounter strong voice, you know it. It almost propels you through the text, exciting your curiosity, making you hungry to read more. Flat voice hits you like a roadblock. Thud. You have to push yourself to keep reading. Your mind wanders. You wish the piece would end already. Following are three short examples. Read each one carefully. Then use the space provided to share your responses.

Example A

Venn Diagrams

A Venn diagram is a kind of diagram found in math textbooks and often used by math teachers. A Venn diagram usually has at least two circles (or other shapes) that overlap to show distinct sets of information. For instance, you could make a Venn diagram about the numbers 1 through 20. One circle could be labeled "Divisible by 2" and the other could be labeled "Divisible by 3." In the part where the circles overlap, you would put numbers like 6, 12, and 18, because they are divisible by both 2 and 3. Some numbers, such as 1 and 11, would not go inside either of the circles.

My reader reaction to Example A:

_____

_____

_____

Example B

Flying Foxes

Flying foxes have lived on Earth for the last 50 million years. They're not really foxes, but they do really fly! Actually, they're fruit bats, mammals that get their name from their fox-like faces. Like their namesakes, they have enormous eyes, which help them pull in every possible bit of light when feeding at night.

Aside from looks, flying foxes have nothing in common with the bushy tailed variety. After all, when was the last time you saw a red fox hanging upside down from a tree branch, chewing on a piece of fruit? Red foxes don't sail through the air, either—but perhaps that's just as well.

Although flying foxes are incredibly capable flyers, it's the landing, as they say, that can kill you. Their landing skills definitely need work. They usually grab onto a branch or crash into bushes to stop. Real foxes may never know the joy of flying, but they won't experience the pain of crashing, either.

My reader reaction to Example B:

_____

_____

_____

Example C

H.G. Wells

Author H.G. Wells wasn't *literally* trying to predict the future in his fantastic stories of space invaders and time travel. He was just using his imagination, along with his understanding of science and technology, to speculate about what life might be like hundreds or even thousands of years after he lived. Born in 1866 in England, he left school at 14 and educated himself by reading everything he could find about science. He eventually became a teacher and even wrote a biology book. But his imagination lured him away from nonfiction and toward the futuristic stories that he loved. In Wells's first novel, *The Time Machine*, he wrote about a scientist who invents a machine for time travel and ends up going 800,000 years into the future.

My reader reaction to Example C:

_____

_____

Voice

Share and Compare

Meet with a partner or in a writing circle to share responses. Following are some questions to ponder as you talk.

- Which writer's voice would keep you reading?
- Where have you read (or heard) similar voices?
- Do any of these voices sound like you?

Sharing Another Confident Voice

Take a few minutes to find a voice-filled passage from *any* nonfiction source. Choose an example that is a few sentences long, and read it carefully to yourself so you feel ready to share it in a way that will bring out all the voice. Then meet in writing circles to share and listen.

I'm the World's Leading Expert

You've heard some confident voices now. You can write that way, too. You can capture your readers' imaginations and win their trust, if you know your topic.

In the real world of writing, writers may spend months researching a topic. We're only going to take about ten minutes. But remember, they're often looking for thousands of intriguing details, while we're only asking you to find three. First, identify your general topic:

_____

Now, read as much of any book chapter or article as you need to uncover three details that will grab a reader's attention and let you sound like an expert. List them here:

1. _____

2. _____

3. _____

You don't know everything about your topic (at least not yet). That's OK. You know enough to write a short paragraph. And as you write, imagine you ARE the world's leading expert on your topic. Let your confidence shine through. Write for ten minutes or more, using your own paper.

Share and Compare

Meet with a partner or in a writing circle to share your paragraphs. Listen for the moment when the confidence shines through the strongest. Share that moment.

A Writer's Questions

You only had time to do **preliminary** research on your topic for this lesson. But what if you stretched your research out over days or weeks? What if it included not only reading but interviews and hands-on experience? Would your voice continue to grow as your knowledge of the topic grew? Why?

Putting It to the Test

On-demand writing doesn't generally call for research as we usually think of it. However, it does sometimes (often unintentionally) call for knowledge that only comes from experience. For example, a question might ask about travel, pets, or heroes who inspire you. Those things may or may not be part of your personal experience. What if you don't have first-hand knowledge? What can you do to create a confident response?

Knowing Your Audience

Writers and people who fish have something very important in common—a need to know their audiences. When you're fishing (assuming you want to catch anything) you'd better understand what you are fishing for. A cutthroat trout is a different audience from a smallmouth bass; they won't go after the same bait. Readers and listeners respond to different things, too. You probably use one voice when talking with your friends and another when talking with your parents. And by adjusting your writing voice even a little, you can increase your chances of hooking your audience dramatically.

Sharing an Example: "Sugarcane Fire"

Here's an example from David Rice's book of short stories, *Crazy Loco.* In this story, "Sugarcane Fire," Romero, a seventh grader, wants to buy tickets to a high school dance for himself and two friends. Unfortunately, he has to purchase them from some high school students who are enjoying making that a little difficult. Listen to the subtle way Romero uses voice to get what he wants.

One of the guys laughed. "You're in junior high. You have no rights." The other students joined in the ha-ha's.

Then I recognized the guy's laugh. A month earlier my English teacher had given the class extra-credit points for watching the high school drama club rehearse a Shakespeare play. Every time one of the actors messed up a line, the guy who was laughing at me now would jump in and make fun of him. And every time, the actor would throw his arms up and respond with the same sentence: "What is this? The Spanish Inquisition?" Then both guys would shout in unison, "Nobody expects the Spanish Inquisition," and all the actors would laugh. I didn't get it, but I knew it worked.

I threw my arms up. "What is this? The Spanish Inquisition?" I said.

The two poker players laughed and answered, "Nobody expects the Spanish Inquisition," and they let me buy three tickets. The girl with the tin box stood up and put out her hand. "That will be nine dollars for you and your dates," she said, smiling. I paid her and walked out happily.

"Sugarcane Fire," from *Crazy Loco*
by David Rice

Reflection

Talk about this passage with a partner or in a writing circle. Following are a few questions to guide your discussion.

- How was Romero feeling inside?
- If he had let those feelings show, what sort of voice would have come out?
- What sort of voice did he use?
- Why did the high school students give him the tickets?

Name   Date

A Different Audience

Romero understood that his audience was older high school boys, and he adjusted his voice accordingly. Suppose the person selling the tickets had been an adult—say, your own teacher. And let's say you're the one requesting the tickets, normally sold ONLY to students in high school. You have three minutes to write a convincing note, and the voice you use could make the difference in whether you get those tickets. Think! Adjust!

_____

_____

_____

_____

_____

_____

Share and Compare

Share your note with a partner or in a writing circle, taking turns reading aloud. What words would you use to describe the voices you hear? Which writer would most likely get the tickets? Share a few notes with your teacher and see!

The Perfect Triangle: Audience, Purpose, and Voice

Strong voice is always lively. But good writers keep audience and purpose in mind so that the voice always suits the occasion.

For this activity, you'll write two persuasive letters to two different audiences. Work with a partner or in a writing circle to choose the topic and the audiences.

Voice

Audiences

There's just one rule here. Your audiences must be very different. Don't write to two teachers, for example. You might write one letter to a teacher or principal and another to a friend who lives out of town.

Topic

Choose a topic you have strong opinions about. Following are some suggestions, but you may choose any controversial topic.

- Gum chewing policy at your school
- Homework expectations
- Cell phone use at school

Letter 1

Dear _____ ,

_____

_____

_____

_____

_____

_____

_____

_____

_____

_____

Letter 2

Dear _____,

_____

_____

_____

_____

_____

_____

_____

_____

Share and Compare

When you finish writing, pick one letter to share with a
partner or in a writing circle. Don't read the greeting or tell
who the letter is going to. See if your partner or your writing
circle members can identify the audience based on the
voice alone.

Name _____   Date _____

A Writer's Questions

You just finished writing letters to two different audiences. Even though the topic for the two letters remained the same, did the purpose actually shift a little? How so?

Putting It to the Test

In on-demand writing, you create a piece for someone you've never met and probably never will meet. Is there a safe voice you should use in this kind of situation? Or is it better to just be yourself and write with the full power of your natural voice, with all the confidence you can muster? Why do you think so?

Conventions and Presentation
Editing Level 1: Conventions
The Triple Threat

Conventions aren't just about rules: put a comma here, insert a semicolon there. Creativity plays a big part, too. Think about the people you know who read aloud really well. You know, the ones who read with voice? You can bet those readers are paying close attention to conventions, because that's one of the best guides they have about how a writer intended his or her writing to be read. In this lesson, we will focus on three conventions that help put voice into writing: the exciting exclamation mark (!), the debonair dash—and the *emphatic italics.* You will use these three conventions (the Triple Threat) to help readers hear the voice in dialogue you write.

A Warm-Up

The exclamation mark is usually one of the first conventions writers learn, so we're betting you can spot one a mile away! And almost everyone knows what italics are, *right?* The dash, however, is often confused with its cousin the hyphen. So let's take one minute to make sure you know the difference. Circle the dash in the following sentence; put a check right above the hyphen:

She was a full-time actor—which amazed everyone who knew how shy she really was.

Here's a quick summary of the hyphen-dash distinction:

- The hyphen can be used to link words (as in *full-time*), create new words (like *hyphen-dash*), or divide a word when you reach the end of a line and have run out of room to finish the word.

- The dash puts emphasis on the words that follow it, shows a new direction in thought, or sets off an interruption:

Just as Jane began her soliloquy—something about the importance of love—her microphone died.

Take a Look

With your teacher's guidance, take a few minutes to skim through several books, looking for examples of dialogue. Keep an extra sharp eye out for dialogue with the following.

- Exclamation marks
- Italics
- Dashes
- A Triple Threat—an example using all three

Another Example

Here's a passage of dialogue from the classic tale *The Wind in the Willows* by Kenneth Grahame. Badger is speaking to Mole about the joy and comfort of underground living, a topic they seem to heartily agree on. Read the passage aloud, letting the conventions guide you.

"That's exactly what I say," he replied. "There's no security, or peace and tranquillity, except underground. And then, if your ideas get larger and you want to expand—why, a dig and a scrape, and there you are! If you feel your house is a bit too big, you stop up a hole or two, and there you are again! No builders, no tradesmen, no remarks passed on you by fellows looking over your wall, and, above all, no *weather*. Look at Rat, now. A couple of feet of flood water, and he's got to move into hired lodgings; uncomfortable, inconveniently situated, and horribly expensive. Take Toad. I say nothing against Toad Hall; quite the best house in these parts, *as* a house. But supposing a fire breaks out—where's Toad? Supposing tiles are blown off, or walls sink or crack, or windows get broken—where's Toad? Supposing the rooms are draughty—I *hate* a draught myself—where's Toad? No, up and out of doors is good enough to roam about and get one's living in; but underground to come back to at last—that's *my* idea of *home!*"

Wind in the Willows
by Kenneth Grahame

Share and Discuss

Go back for one more look and circle or highlight any conventions that helped you figure out just how to read this passage. Would you have used additional *italics* or exclamation marks? Do you "hear" where they should go when you read aloud, even if author Kenneth Grahame didn't put them in?

The Triple Threat Conversation

Now that you have warmed up with the passage from Kenneth Grahame, it's time to practice the Triple Threat with a conversation that currently contains no dashes, italics, or exclamation marks. Read it carefully. Then decide if some additional conventions could make interpretive reading easier. Be careful, though. You don't want to create too! much! excitement! or—too—many—interruptions—or *too much emphasis.*

Chandra slipped off her gloves and reached into her backpack looking for her phone. "I'm freezing, and the bus is late. I don't even think it's coming. When I find my phone, I'm texting my dad. Maybe he will pick us up."

"Don't send a message yet." Alex put his hand on her backpack to slow down her search. "You're right, it's cold, but the bus is always a little late. The last time you called your dad, he seemed, oh, just a tiny bit irritated. I'm sure the bus will be here. There it is now. See how patient I was? That's a sign of maturity."

Chandra ended the search for her phone. "Maturity? Ha. You're just an old, a very old, man living inside the body of a boring thirteen year old."

Share and Compare

Meet with a partner to compare your work. Did you use conventions the same way? If there were differences, try reading both revisions to see which you like better.

A Writer's Questions

When characters in a book are speaking, do they sometimes break conventional rules? As a writer do you need to do this to make your dialogue sound authentic? Can breaking rules to bring out voice be just as hard as following them?

Editing Level 2: Presentation
The Play's the Thing

What is the difference between dialogue in a novel and dialogue in a play? Performance! The dialogue in a play should be acted out. Actors don't just stand around like mannequins, speaking their lines. They move. They show feelings. And they interact with other characters onstage. The playwright helps by describing the setting and offering directions to guide actors' movements—even gestures or facial expressions. In this lesson, you'll get a chance to think and write like a playwright. That puts you in pretty good company. After all, a famous playwright gave us the title for this lesson. (Who was it?)

A Warm-Up

Here's the dialogue from the first part of this lesson. We rewrote it as a play. Look at it carefully with a partner or in a writing circle. Talk about any differences you see between this and the first version, and note them in the space provided.

(Scene 1: Two friends, Chandra and Alex, are waiting for the school bus on a city sidewalk. It's a chilly morning, about 7 a.m. No one else is around.)

Chandra: (looking impatient, stomping her feet and staring down the highway hopefully, then slipping off her gloves and reaching into her backpack as if looking for something)
I'm freezing!!! The bus is late—I don't even think it's *coming*. When I find *my* phone, I'm texting *my* dad. Maybe *he* will pick us up.

Alex: (smiling broadly and putting one hand on Chandra's backpack as if to stop her search) Don't send a message *yet.* You're right, it's cold, but the bus is *always* a *little* late. The last time you called your dad, he seemed, oh, just a *tiny bit* irritated. I'm sure the bus will be here—there it *is!* See how *patient* I was? That's a sign of *maturity.*

Chandra: (taking her hand out of the backpack and looking at the bus, deliberately avoiding Alex's gaze) *Maturity?!?* Ha! You're just an old—a *very* old—man living inside the body of a *boring* thirteen year old!

Differences we noticed in this version:

1. _____
2. _____
3. _____
4. _____
5. _____

Presentable or Not Presentable: That Is the Question!

Have you ever attended a play, acted in one, or helped design a set? Can you name any famous playwrights? Maybe you're familiar with William Shakespeare and his play *Romeo and Juliet.* (If not, you likely will be soon.)

But here's a play we doubt you've heard of, so we dusted it off for you—or at least a part of it. This play by Percival Wilde is called *His Return.* (Look up Mr. Wilde on the web if you'd like to know more.) We have included just enough to give you a feel for what is happening and to see an authentic script the way actors might see it.

As you read through the script, think about the important elements that would help you as an actor or as a director.

His Return

A Play in One-Act
By Percival Wilde

Characters:

Helen Hartley

John Hartley

Sylvia Best

A Maid

Time:

The Summer of 1918

The nicely furnished boudoir in Mrs. Hartley's home in a small Northwestern town. There are three doors. The central one leads into the hall; the one on the right into the interior of the house; the one on the left into a bathroom. There is the furniture one would expect; a dressing table, a chaise-lounge, two or three dainty chairs, and a pier-glass at one side. On the dressing table are two large framed photographs.

At the rise of the curtain the stage is empty. There is a pause. Then there enters John Hartley, a man of thirty-five or forty, dressed in a Canadian uniform.

He is very much excited. He is returning home after an absence of years. He enters as if he expects to find his wife here. She is not. He is disappointed, but he takes visible pleasure in going about the room, identifying the many familiar objects which it contains. He stops abruptly at the sight of two portraits on his wife's dressing table, one of him, one of her. He takes up her picture, deeply affected, and kisses it.

There is a pause. Then he hears steps coming and straightens up expectantly.

The maid enters.

THE MAID: (looking at him in surprise) How—how did you get in here?

HARTLEY: (smiling) Why, I walked upstairs.

THE MAID: Yes, yes, I know that. But how did you get into the house? I didn't hear the bell ring.

HARTLEY: I opened the door. (As she looks her surprise, he shows her a latchkey.) With this.

THE MAID: (with sudden comprehension) O—oh! Then you—you're the master! (Hartley nods and smiles.) You're Captain Hartley! I'm so glad to see you! Why, I've heard all about you, and your medals, and being wounded, for three years! (timidly) Might I—might I shake hands with you, Captain?

HARTLEY: Why, of course! (He shakes hands.)

THE MAID: (rubbing her hand delightedly) I never thought I'd shake hands with a real hero!

. . . .

And here is where we're going to bring our curtain down (even though the play actually does go on).

Checklist

What important elements did you notice in this script? Start with our list, and add anything else we might have forgotten.

- ☐ Title, author
- ☐ Cast list (also known as *dramatis personae*—persons of the drama)
- ☐ Description of the setting
- ☐ Stage directions (showing actors what to do)
- ☐ Name of the character who is speaking
- ☐ Appropriate easy-to-read font

☐ Effective use of italics or other conventions to bring out voice

☐ Authentic dialogue that makes characters sound like real people

☐ Good overall presentation (layout, spacing, margins) to make reading easy

Other things we noticed:

1. _____

2. _____

3. _____

Share and Compare

Share your thoughts with another writing circle, or with the class as a whole. If you were an actor, would you find this script easy to work with? What if you were the director?

A Writer's Questions
Are presentation and layout issues more or less important in a play script than in a novel? Why?

Presentation Matters

For this part of the lesson, you get to be the playwright. You don't have to start from scratch, and you will have support (from a partner or your writing circle). Start by choosing a scene you'd like to work on. You might choose any of the following.

• The next scene from the play *His Return* by Percival Wilde (this will be your version, not Mr. Wilde's)

- The next scene from the story of Chandra and Alex (you decide when and where this scene occurs, and give the play a title)
- Any original scene featuring dialogue between two characters you invent for this play

Your goal is to make sure the actors have all they would need to use your script, if they were really performing it as a play onstage. Use our checklist to help you, and rehearse your play to check it out.

HINT: Don't forget to assign one person the role of director.

Checklist

☐ Title, author

☐ Cast list (dramatis personae)

☐ Description of the setting (time and place)

☐ Stage directions (showing actors what to do)

☐ Name of the character who is speaking

☐ Appropriate easy-to-read font

☐ Effective use of italics or other conventions to bring out voice

☐ Authentic dialogue that makes characters sound like real people

☐ Good overall presentation (layout, spacing, margins) to make reading easy

Plus, the following things we thought of ourselves:

1. _____

2. _____

3. _____

Sample Paper 11
Score for Voice _____

Annapurna: One of the 14

There are fourteen mountain peaks, each over 8,000 meters tall, in the Himalayan mountains on the border between China and India. Annapurna is one of those fourteen. At 26,545 feet, it is the tenth highest mountain in the world. It was first climbed in 1950 by Maurice Herzog and Louis Lachenal.

The name *Annapurna,* translated from Sanskrit, means Goddess of the Harvests. The literal translation is "full of food." It is a very dangerous mountain to climb with the highest mortality (death) rate of any of the 8,000 meter peaks. There have been 130 successful climbs and 53 deaths. Actually, Annapurna is made up of several peaks, with six of them higher than 7,000 meters.

Mountain climbing is exciting and dangerous. You can suffer a fatal fall or die of hypothermia. According to one study, mountain climbers can also lose brain cells and weaken their motor skills if they climb at high elevations.

Annapurna continues to attract climbers because of its mystery and beauty and danger.

Sources

Maurice Herzog. *Annapurna.* New York, NY: The Lyons Press, 1997.

Potterfield, Peter. Himalayan Quest: Ed Viesturs Summits All Fourteen 8,000-Meter Giants. From National Geographic, 2009.

Messner, Reinhold. 2000. *Annapurna: 50 Years of Expeditions in the Death Zone.* Published in Seattle, WA by The Mountaineers Books, 2000.

http://well.blogs.nytimes.com/2008/10/20/mountain-climbing-bad-for-the-brain/ New York Times on-line Oct. 20, 2008 Mountain Climbing Bad for the Brain by Tara Parker-Pope

Name _____ Date _____

Sample Paper 12

Score for Voice _____

The Little Black Dress

Coco Chanel, the legendary fashion designer, once said, "A girl should be two things: classy and fabulous." Though she died in 1971, anyone who pays attention to high-fashion knows that Coco Chanel's influential words and designs changed the fashion industry forever. Her classic Chanel No. 5 perfume, first introduced in 1924, continues to sell even today, at the rate of one bottle every 30 seconds. Purses and handbags bearing the distinctive "CC" logo are sold in shops and boutiques around the world. But it is the "little black dress" for which she is most famous. Coco's simple black dress design revolutionized fashion.

If you have ever watched one of the reality shows about fashion designers, you know that high fashion is often about wild ideas, taking chances, and starting trends. Today, people often interpret that to mean glitz and glamour, wild colors, feathers, unusual fabrics like ostrich skin, and sequins or jewels. Chanel had a different vision altogether. But make no mistake: in 1926, Chanel's black dress seemed wild and chancy.

At that time, women's dresses were long and layered, and covered just about everything. Black was not a color for parties or social events. Women wore black to mourn or attend funerals. Chanel's design crashed headlong through that tradition. Her dress was chic and elegant, a simple, form-fitting sleeveless black sheath, cut barely above the knee. Arms and legs showing! How scandalous! Women loved it—and bought it. In fact, they bought millions.

Name   Date

This little black dress, with a few variations, is still the ultimate in high fashion, and will be forever. Add a few accessories, jewelry and shoes, and a woman can wear this dress almost anywhere fashion matters. Coco Chanel's little black dress has become the classy, fabulous answer for women faced with the question, "What should I wear?"

Sources

Karbo, Karen. *The Gospel According to Coco Chanel: Life Lessons from the World's Most Elegant Woman.* Guilford, CT: The Globe Pequot Press, 2009.

The Style Strategy: A Less-Is-More Approach to Staying Chic and Shopping Smart by Nina Garcia. New York, NY: HarperCollins, 2009.

http://coololdstuff.com/coco.html Coco Chanel: Innovator and Icon by Aime Joseph

http://en.wikipedia.org/wiki/Chanel

http://allwomenstalk.com/fashion-icons-ae-7-things-what-you-should-know-about-coco-chanel/

http://www.brainyquote.com/quotes/authors/c/coco_chanel.html

Revising Checklist for Voice

- [ ] I feel strongly about this topic, so it was EASY to show that. OR
- [ ] I plan to change my topic to _____
- [ ] I know a LOT about this topic, so I sound confident. OR
- [ ] I plan to get more information from _____
- [ ] I read this aloud to myself, and it sounds *just like* me.
- [ ] _____ rated my writing:

1	2	3	4	5	6

- [ ] I think a reader would *love* to share this aloud.
- [ ] I have highlighted any parts that need to be stronger. I plan to
  - [ ] add details to make the writing more interesting.
  - [ ] say what I *really* think and feel (write as if I *mean it*).
  - [ ] use different words to give the writing life or energy.
- [ ] This is my purpose: _____

  My voice is ___ a good fit for this purpose ___ not quite right yet

- [ ] Here's how I want readers to feel: _____
- [ ] My voice will make them feel this way.
- [ ] I used punctuation carefully so that when someone reads this aloud, it will sound just the way I intended it to sound.

> **Note** Your voice is really YOU on the page. Are you there? Are you at home in your writing? Do you speak right *to* readers?

Word Choice

Suppose you carried your money around in a big jar. And every time you wanted to buy something, you'd just reach in, grab a fistful, and scatter it on the counter. Sometimes you might come close to the right amount. Most of the time, though, you'd probably be miles off—leaving the cashier either delighted or dismayed.

Surprisingly, many writers use this very approach with words. They reach for the first words that come to mind and toss them at readers—sometimes using too many or not enough, sometimes using the wrong words altogether. Whether you're making purchases or writing, the "correct change" is always appreciated.

In this unit, you'll learn ways of being right on the money with Word Choice. You'll practice

- recognizing shades of meaning and using a thesaurus wisely.

- finding the words that are just right for your purpose.

- revising in stages—first de-cluttering, then adding vivid detail.

- energizing writing with strong verbs.

Sample Paper 13

Score for Word Choice _____

A Good Place to Visit, But . . .

Although I watch more than my fair share of television, apparently I don't watch enough medical shows—the kind with eccentric doctors and dedicated nurses. Otherwise, I would have been prepared for the arctic blast that awaited me in the OR (operating room).

People recall different things about surgery—fasting ahead of time, wearing skimpy gowns, waiting to get it over with. Mostly, I recall wishing someone would turn on the heat. I wasn't expecting tropical warmth—but I didn't anticipate shivering until my teeth clashed. It was so icy in the operating room that I thought I saw snowflakes. Everything was stainless steel, adding to the wintry atmosphere. (I could have sworn that the doctors and nurses were wearing parkas and mittens, and that I could see the steam from their breath, but this was probably a side effect of the anesthesia and pain medication.)

The doctors kept asking me how "we" were doing, and while *they* seemed to be doing fine, *my* lips were frozen, so I just rolled my eyes and groaned. As long as you can still make noise, doctors think there is hope. They gave me an IV before rolling me into surgery. This would allow them, they claimed, to pump painkillers and antibiotics into my system without having to wake me in the night. (That sounded good—except they woke me hourly anyway to take my temperature and check my blood pressure.)

Once you're thoroughly frozen, they say you don't feel much pain—but I guess they didn't want to rely *totally* on that approach. They administered enough anesthetic during surgery to knock out a buffalo, so I woke up with blurry vision and a mouth that tasted as if I had been munching on rotten prairie grass. I could not get up to brush my teeth, and in fact, I could hardly raise myself off the pillow.

The nurses told me I could go home as soon as I visited the bathroom on my own and ate something without throwing up. Both sounded as likely as bungee jumping off the Empire State Building. But motivation to get out of a hospital is very strong. (No heat. No sleep. Bad food. *No one* wants to stay.) I felt like one of those guys on the TV reality shows who has to down a dozen live worms to get a prize. I willed myself up onto my feet and propelled myself across the frigid linoleum, and got the prize: freedom and a ride home. Once there, I bundled in as many layers as I could get on and rolled myself in front of the fire, just soaking up the heat and enjoying the beauty of the flames. If you are ever in need of surgery, follow my advice: Do your best to schedule it for the summer. Or sneak in your space heater.

Name   Date

Sample Paper 14
Score for Word Choice _____
Most Embarrassing Moment

My most embarrassing moment happened when my sister had her new boyfriend over for dinner. I had made dinner because my mom had to work late. It wasn't a problem. I made frozen lasagna, and it turned out fine. That was not the embarrassing part. I had set the table nicely, too. That was not the embarrassing part, either. Everything looked really great. I even had flowers on the table. They looked nice, too. Then I went to turn on the music. That was when things went bad.

I was working on a project for social studies, and I was making a recording of songs. That wouldn't have been so bad except that I was singing the songs. So when I turned on the music, on came me singing really loudly. I am just an OK singer, not a great singer. My sister looked mad. I thought my sister was going to toss the lasagna right at me. Her boyfriend got this look on his face. Nobody said anything. I turned on a radio station as fast as I could. I don't even remember which one because I was so embarrassed that I just pressed a button. It was not a good experience.

Word Choice

So the READER...

The WRITER...
chooses words with just the
right shade of meaning.

_____
_____
_____

So the READER...

The WRITER...
uses sensory words
and phrases.

_____
_____
_____

So the READER...

The WRITER...
uses powerful verbs.

_____
_____
_____

So the READER...

The WRITER...
keeps it concise.

_____
_____
_____

Shades of Meaning

Have you ever collected rocks, sports cards, seashells, or anything? If you're like most collectors, you're proud of your collection and love adding to it. Many writers—maybe you're one— also love to collect words. They add to their collections by reading, conversing, keeping word lists in journals—and sometimes browsing through a good thesaurus. A vast word collection allows you to select words with the perfect shade of meaning to convey your idea. That kind of precision gives your word choice power.

Sharing an Example: *Hope Was Here*

Read the following passage from Joan Bauer's book *Hope Was Here*. In this passage Hope, a self-described "word person," is using her thesaurus to help her work out her feelings.

I took out my Roget's thesaurus, which lists words that have the same meaning. If you're a word person like me, you can't live without one. Say you're trying to get an idea across, like *Gleason Beal is a thief.* You can look up the word "thief" in the thesaurus and come up with a slew of even better slams to help you work out your intense feelings.

Gleason Beal is a . . .

. . . robber.

. . . stealer.

. . . purloiner (I like that one).

. . . larcenist.

. . . pilferer.

. . . poacher.

. . . swindler.

I flipped to the H section.

Hope is . . .

. . . belief.

. . . credence.

. . . faith.

. . . trust.

. . . confidence.

. . . assurance.

I lay on the bed, holding the thesaurus, trying to live up

to my name.

Hope Was Here
by Joan Bauer

Reflection

If, like Hope, you face lots of word choices, how do you pick the one word that's just right? How do the various synonyms for *thief* differ? Which ones work best for someone who steals your money? How about someone who steals your heart? Discuss this with a partner or in a writing circle and prepare to share some thoughts with the class.

Also look at the synonyms for *hope*. How do they differ? Which one do you think goes best with the name *Hope?*

Using Your Thesaurus

To look up synonyms (words with the same or similar meaning) in a thesaurus, it helps to know what part of speech you're looking for—noun or verb, for example.

Is *hope* a noun or a verb in each of these sentences? Talk with your partner to decide.

- Our soccer skills are low, but our hope for a win is high.
- I hope it snows tomorrow.

Use your thesaurus to find three synonyms for *hope* used as a verb:

1. _____

2. _____

3. _____

Choose one of the three synonyms you found and look up that word in the thesaurus. Write down two or more synonyms for your word:

_____

Shades of *Hope*

Now that you know a few synonyms for *hope*, you're in a good position to express an idea in more than one way. Read the following sentence and think about other ways to express the idea without using the word *hope*. It's fine to reword the sentence, add details, start it differently, or express the idea more strongly. Remember—this is about shades of meaning.

I hope we win the game.

Write three more ways to say—more or less—the same thing:

1. _____

2. _____

3. _____

Shades of *Big*

Here are some synonyms for *big*. If you were going to put these synonyms for *big* in order, which three would be the "biggest" of the *big* words? Put stars by those three. It's fine to work with a partner as you do this.

- huge
- gigantic
- gargantuan
- enormous
- mammoth
- vast
- whopping
- large
- humongous
- sprawling
- giant
- oversized
- expansive
- spacious

As you know, synonyms do not have *exactly* the same meaning. You can't just plunk any old word in the blank. Read these sentences carefully to see if the writer chose a good synonym for *big* in each case. If not, cross out the **bold word** and write a better choice right above it. **NOTE:** You do not have to use a word from the list. If you have a better choice, use it!

1. Herman managed to finish the **vast** pizza.

2. They owned **spacious** acreage in Texas.

3. **Large** waves pounded the shore.

4. The dog had **expansive** feet.

5. That's some **oversized** fish you caught!

6. Her **sprawling** hat blocked my view.

Share and Compare

Compare your choices with those of your classmates. Did you hear words the same way? If you cannot agree, use a dictionary and a thesaurus to zero in on the meaning of any given word. And if any of these words are new to you, be sure to add them to the word list in your writing journal.

Creating Meaning

Let's say you're writing a mystery set in 19th century England. In your opening scene, the heroine Dorcas is running from her small house on a cliff (heroines love living on cliffs) down a dark path to a tiny village at the edge of the sea. She plans to warn her friend that a ship carrying a particularly menacing person is approaching.

Read the story carefully, paying attention to the **bold blue** words. With a partner or in your writing circle, use your thesaurus to find a synonym that might work better than each of these words. Feel free to reword any sentences—or add original details. **HINT:** Imagine that this story is going to become a film. Make it exciting, vivid—and mysterious.

The Ship
Chapter 1

Dorcas looked up at the sky. Dark clouds were forming in the west—a bad storm was coming. She took her hat from the peg on the wall and pulled it down over her ears—then stepped out. The wind shut the door behind her. It circled around her, almost taking the coat right off her back.

Holding her coat, Dorcas started down the dark path. The wind was blowing—so there was no point lighting a candle. She couldn't see a thing—tree roots came up everywhere, and sharp rocks pushed into her feet. If only she could reach the village in time. Dr. Perfidy, the most unpleasant person ever to sail the seas, was about to dock at their port! She was worried, but there was no time to think of herself. Lightning shone, and in the light, Dorcas saw the slim outline of the ship's mast and sails. She stopped worrying about falling and ran down the narrow path, her feet hitting the dirt, and her heart beating with every step.

Share and Compare

Share your revision with another group or with the whole class. As you listen to other versions, record any words you especially want to remember. Think about the meaning of each word and about the mood it creates.

A Writer's Question

As you've seen in this lesson, words aren't just about literal meaning. They're also about mood. Suppose you wanted to write a light, happy piece showing that Dorcas had been waiting and wishing for the ship to come in so she could meet someone she loved and missed. How would your word choice change?

Putting It to the Test

Let's say you're in a writing assessment and you need a synonym for *good*. You have a thesaurus handy and it shows more than 20 synonyms for this word. Can you just pick any one of them? If not, how will you know which one is right for your particular sentence?

Words to Fit the Purpose

Have you ever glanced at a legal contract—or a technical manual? If so, you know that such documents rely on precise word choice and specific terminology to make meaning unambiguous. This kind of word choice is very different from what you would expect in a movie script, poem, or picture book. And that's because they are written for totally different purposes. As you will see in this lesson, good word choice sometimes means striving for unmistakable clarity—and it sometimes means creating word pictures in the reader's mind. Both are important goals—but they're not interchangeable.

Two Examples—Two Purposes

The following two examples show how much word choice can fluctuate with purpose. Example 1 is from a cookbook. The recipe is written with clear, precise terms to help the reader understand *exactly* how to bake a cake. Example 2 is a descriptive piece, in which the writer chooses words that will convey his passion for the beach.

Example 1

Read the following passage carefully and <u>underline</u> any examples of clear wording that would help a reader know *exactly* how to make a chocolate cake. We underlined two examples to give you the idea.

Delectably-Chocolate Chocolate Cake

1. <u>Preheat</u> the oven to 350 degrees. <u>Liberally grease and flour</u> two 9-inch round baking pans. Put these pans aside for now.

2. In a large bowl, whisk together the sugar, flour, cocoa, baking powder, baking soda, and salt until everything is evenly blended. Once mixed, add in the eggs, milk, oil, and vanilla. With an electric mixer, beat batter on medium speed until thoroughly mixed, about 2 minutes. Scrape sides of the bowl with a rubber spatula as needed. The batter should be thick and blended. Pour contents into prepared pans.

3. Bake 30 to 35 minutes. A wooden toothpick inserted into the center should come out clean. Let cool 10 minutes. Remove from pans to wire racks, cool completely, frost, and enjoy!

Example 2

This time as you read, <u>underline</u> any descriptive wording that helps you picture the scene—or understand the writer's feelings. Again, we underlined two examples to give you the idea.

The Ocean

For as long as I can remember, the beach has been *the* place I wanted to spend my summers. <u>I loved combing the surf for sun-bleached sand dollars</u>, pants rolled up under my knees, thick, wet sand oozing between my toes. Later, as the sun melted into the sea, we'd overeat, stuffing ourselves with butter-dripping clams steamed in salty water, then golden marshmallows toasted over a driftwood fire.

It was here, in the ocean's pounding surf and in the salty tidal waters of nearby rivers, that I learned to fish and to love paddling around in our family's red, weather-beaten canoe. No matter how many times I follow the familiar tree-lined road from my house in town to the ocean, I still love that moment when we crest the hill, pop out of the forest and—just like that—there it is. My breath catches, as if I'm seeing that impossibly vast expanse of water for the first time. Regardless of the weather—eye blinding sunshine or clouds thick as cotton batting—I get the same lump in my throat, and I hear the tide even before I actually *see* the ocean.

Share and Compare

Meet with a partner or in a writing circle to share your underlined words from the two examples. Identify your favorites. Then talk about *different kinds* of good word choice. What kinds of words was the writer of the chocolate cake recipe reaching for? How about the writer of the piece about the ocean? Is it appropriate for their word choices to be very different?

Name _____ Date _____

Warming Up

Following are two sentences that need your help. In each case, the writer has settled for bland language—or omitted details that would fill in the picture by answering readers' questions. Read each sentence carefully. Think about the writer's *purpose.* Then

- underline vague words.
- rewrite the sentence, using vivid words that fit the purpose well.

Don't be afraid to invent. You're a writer—that's your job. We did one example to show you what we had in mind.

Example Revision

Before: Leslie <u>went</u> down to the lake.

Purpose: To set the stage for an adventure story

After: Just at dawn, Leslie slipped out of bed and headed quietly to the edge of the small mountain lake to watch the trout jumping.

HINT: Remember, this isn't JUST about replacing a weak word with a stronger one. It's also about using language that goes with the writer's purpose.

Your Turn

1. **Before:** The views are good.

   Purpose: To create a compelling brochure for visitors to New York

   After: _____

   _____

   _____

2. **Before:** The unusual sea creature does some interesting things to get food.

   Purpose: To open Chapter 1 of a fourth grade science textbook

   After: _____

   _____

   _____

Word Choice

Name _____   Date _____

Share and Compare

Meet with a partner to share your revised sentences. Take turns reading your new sentences aloud. Even though you reached for different words (and probably different ideas), did you manage to give clarity and voice to your writing? Did your words suit the purpose?

Ready, Set . . . *Reach!*

It's time to start a draft of your own. Take a minute to decide if you'd rather write

- a how-to piece (like the cake recipe),

- a description (like the paragraphs about the beach), OR

- a poem (on any original idea of your own).

Regardless of your topic or purpose, take a few minutes to create a word web. Place your main idea in the middle of the web, then brainstorm and write as many words or phrases as you can think of to bring readers inside your thinking. Choose words that will help readers either (1) follow your directions, (2) picture something you are describing, or (3) tune in to your feelings. Add as many circles as you need.

Name .... Date ....

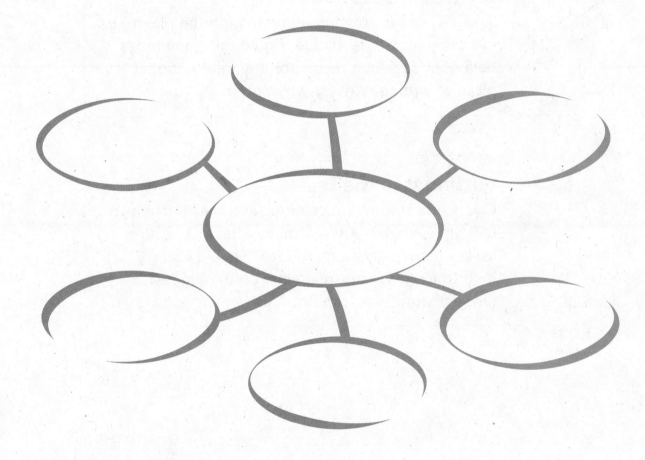

As soon as you finish your web, begin writing—and keep writing for 10-15 minutes. Keep the ideas flowing. Have a conversation with your reader.

Share and Compare

Meet with a partner or in a writing circle to share your drafts. As each writer finishes reading, share a favorite word or phrase from his or her writing and talk about the match between word choice and purpose. Is it strong?

A Writer's Questions

A writer who is creating a poem might be playful or even daring with language. Could this sometimes be a good idea in a recipe, or any informational piece of writing? Why or why not?

Putting It to the Test

Give some writers a thesaurus, and they'll use it to look up every other word they write. In a writing assessment, is this a good idea? Should you try hard to impress your readers with the biggest, fanciest words you can find?

The One-Two Revision Punch

Maybe you've heard of a one-two punch. It's a quick succession of punches boxers sometimes use to take down an opponent. Revisers have a one-two punch of their own. It calls for de-cluttering with the first punch and then adding important detail with the second. Sometimes revising in stages not only makes the process easier to manage, but it gives the writer valuable time to reflect on how best to make a piece of writing stronger.

The First Punch: De-clutter!

Details are important to good writing, but clutter—unneeded words—can bury a message alive. Clutter usually takes one of two forms: repetition of an expression or idea, or empty words that simply don't say anything important. Read the example titled "Good Shot!" carefully, looking and listening for clutter.

Good Shot!

My mother is a doctor of pediatrics. This means that she is a pediatrician, a doctor who works with children. As a pediatrician who sees a lot of children, she often has funny things happen to her in her office. At least a couple times a week, she comes home with hilarious stories of her patients doing funny things. Just the other day, my mom told me a story after coming home from a day of working with children. This one patient, a child around the age of five, had to get a shot. A lot of children are not crazy about shots, and as it happened, this particular child didn't like shots at all. In fact, he had what you could call a bad case of "shot phobia," or a real fear of getting a shot of any kind. When this child, a boy I'll call Theo, heard the word *shot* come out of his doctor's (my mother's) mouth, he began to scream. His scream was not an ordinary "you-scared-me" scream. No, Theo's scream was a wild, crazy, jungle-animal, "there's-a-python-after-me" loud, long, blood-curdling scream that caused my mom's nurse, who works in the same office, to drop the hypodermic needle she was holding. The hypodermic needle did not drop down to the hard, tiled floor where it would have shattered into hundreds of pieces. No, this hypodermic needle bounced off the cushioned examination table, where the patients sit, turned over in the air one time, and landed in a very soft place. The soft place where it landed was Theo's behind. Theo, who had been screaming, stopped screaming and stared at the nurse. The nurse, who had been trying to give him a shot, just reached down and finished off the shot. It's hard to believe, but, unbelievably, Theo began to laugh. When *my mom* told me this story, I had to laugh, too.

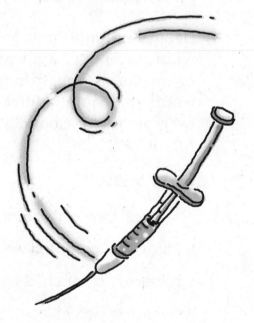

My Response

Which of the following best describes your response to "Good Shot!"?

- [ ] It's a good balance of detail and concise writing.
- [ ] It's a little cluttery, but if I hadn't been looking carefully for clutter, I wouldn't have noticed.
- [ ] It's ridiculously wordy! It could be cut in half!

Partner Up to Pare Down

Work with a partner to revise "Good Shot!" First discuss the piece. Does it need a little trim or a major overhaul? Then work together to de-clutter, reading the piece aloud sentence by sentence and deciding what to cut. **HINT:** After slicing away, you may need to reword some sentences to smooth the flow.

Share and Compare

Compare our revision with yours. Did you use the same strategy? As you can see, we did not add any details. We just cut clutter, trimming the original 315-word draft down to a skinny but powerful 132 words (title not included).

Good Shot!

My mother is a pediatrician, a doctor who works with children, and she often has funny stories about her work. The other day, a five-year-old patient named Theo had to get a shot. Theo has "shot phobia," and as soon as he heard the *word shot*, he let out a crazy "there's-a-python-after-me" blood-curdling scream that caused the nurse to drop the hypodermic needle. It didn't land on the tiled floor, where it would have shattered. It bounced off the cushioned examination table, turned over in the air one time, and landed in a very soft place—Theo's behind. Theo instantly stopped screaming and stared at the nurse, who reached down and finished off the shot. Then, unbelievably, Theo began to laugh. When *my mom* told me this story, I had to laugh, too.

Name _____ Date _____

Put a check (√) next to the sentence that best describes your comparison of our version to yours:

☐ We cut *even more* clutter—our story is short but complete.

☐ We cut almost as much clutter—and our story is similar.

☐ We couldn't bear to cut anything. It was all just *so good*!

☐ We actually *added* words, creating a longer, stronger story.

The One-Two Punch: De-clutter, Re-build

Following is another piece that needs your help. This time, you'll revise in steps, working on your own first. Follow this plan:

- Read the passage called "Shedding Pounds" to get the main idea.
- Read it again, pencil in hand, deleting clutter.
- Read it a third time, inserting two or three vivid details that add meaning and voice.

HINT: It is fine to reword anything. We double spaced to give you revision room. You do NOT need to recopy anything.

Shedding Pounds

Both my parents, my mom and my dad, are on this diet, or as my dad would say, "shedding some unneeded pounds." I think it's good they're trying to do this because it's good for them in the long run to be in better shape and more fit. I am also really happy that this diet does not require them to eat a bunch of wacky, strange food that I wouldn't want to eat. As a matter of fact, they are now eating a lot more foods that are good for them.

This means eating less junk food and more fruits and vegetables. This is OK with me because I've always been a fruit and vegetable person. That may seem strange for a kid to eat a lot of fruits and vegetables, but I do. My parents are also trying to exercise more by doing things like walking, biking, yoga, and even running. Fortunately, allowing me to beat them at basketball is another form of exercise we can enjoy as a whole family, and even though they always lose, they at least get a workout! And that's a good thing!

Share and Compare

Share your revision with a partner or in a writing circle. See how many revision strategies you can list. (Add more numbers if you need to.) If any person on your team tried a given strategy, list it here:

1. _____

2. _____

3. _____

4. _____

5. _____

6. _____

Name .... Date ....

A Writer's Question

Suppose a writer has trouble telling the clutter from the good stuff. (Ever have this problem when cleaning out your closet?) What advice would you offer?

Putting It to the Test

In an on-demand writing situation, you often do not have time to go back and cross out words or sentences. Can you think of any strategy you could use to keep clutter from accumulating in your writing in the first place?

Harness the Power of Verbs

nothing is more important to strong word choice than powerful verbs. Verbs are the engine of writing. They put mental pictures into motion. Of course, as you likely suspect, you cannot insert any old verb into any old slot. There's a big difference between climbing the stairs and bounding up the stairs, or between shrugging and sulking, smiling and grimacing, reading a book and ripping through it. In this lesson, we invite you to come up with some verbal nuances of your own—using your thesaurus to help you.

Sharing an Example: Gulliver's Travels

In the following passage from the novel *Gulliver's Travels* by Jonathan Swift, Lemuel Gulliver has just washed ashore after a terrible storm. Upon waking, he finds tiny strings tying him firmly to the ground. As you read the passage, look and listen for verbs that help you picture the scene—or just contribute to the energy of the passage. Underline each one you find.

I felt something alive moving on my left leg, which advancing gently forward over my chest, came almost up to my chin. When bending my eyes downward, I perceived it to be a human creature not six inches high, with a bow and arrow in his hands and a quiver at his back. In the meantime, I felt at least forty more of

the same kind following the first. I roared so loud that they all ran
back in a fright, and some of them were hurt with the falls they
got leaping from my sides upon the ground.

At length, struggling to get loose, I had the fortune to break
the strings and wrench out the pegs that fastened my left arm to
the ground.

Gulliver's Travels
by Jonathan Swift

Share and Compare

Meet with a partner or in a writing circle to share the verbs
you underlined. Did you mark the very same words? Did you
mark *every single verb*—or did some stand out as especially
important? Are there any you would replace with other
options?

The One-Liner Warm-Up

Time to reach for that thesaurus again. (You're becoming
an expert in using it!) In the following sentences, we've put
some verbs in **bold print**. That doesn't mean they're bold
verbs, however; in fact, most are downright wimpy. Use your
imagination *and* thesaurus to replace each wimpy verb with
one that creates a vivid movie in the reader's mind. Work
with a partner or in a writing circle.

1. We **moved away** as the wild dog **ran** toward us.

2. As the groom slipped and **went** into the cake, a huge laugh
   came from the bride.

3. The enormous eagle **saw** the mouse before we did, and
   within two seconds, **came** down and **took** it.

4. The silent snake **moved** through the grass, **coming**

alarmingly close to the campers' bare feet.

5. The thief **walked** away with his prize, **looking back** over

his shoulder.

Share and Compare

Share your revisions in a writing circle—or with the whole
class. Talk about why you chose some of the verbs you did.
What kind of picture does each one create? Do verbs also
affect mood?

Paving the Way for Verbs

While verbs are important in all writing, they're vital in any
writing involving action—such as the earlier passage from
Gulliver's Travels. For this practice, we want you to choose a
writing topic in which action plays an important role. You do
NOT have to write about sports in order to include action.
Even weeding the garden can be very active—and perhaps
you're even into "extreme weeding." (Who isn't?) Choose your
own topic or use our list to help you think of an idea:

★ My own topic: _____

_____

OR . . .

- Any sports moment (game or practice) you recall well
- Any chore involving physical motion
- A wild ride of any kind
- Violent weather
- Dancing
- Cooking

To see if your topic is a good one, close your eyes for just
one minute and picture the "movie" playing in your mind.
Can you think of three or four verbs to describe what's
happening? If so, you've made an outstanding choice.

Roughing It

Take five minutes to prewrite. List details, make a sketch, or make a word web featuring power verbs that go with your topic.

When you finish, take ten minutes (or more) to write a rough draft. Be SURE you double space, allowing room for revision later. Write quickly—and pack in the action.

Revising with Verbs in Mind

Read your rough draft through carefully. Underline any verbs you find. Are they all just right? If some could be stronger, use your thesaurus to find a good synonym (or synonym for a synonym). If you can't decide, write down some possibilities and ask a partner or your writing circle team to help with your choice.

Share and Compare

Share your revised draft with partners or in writing circles—and ask for help if you need it. As each writer shares, listen for verbs. Which ones stand out? Write your favorite on an index card, fold it, and hand it to the writer after he or she shares. Do NOT read the cards until everyone has shared.

A Writer's Questions

Let's say a sports columnist decides to use verbs and nouns as the foundation of all writing—and to leave out most modifiers (adjectives and adverbs). Do you think this barebones writing would be effective? Or would something be missing? Can you find a sports column (or any writing example) to back up your opinion?

Putting It to the Test: Class Discussion

Is it possible to insert strong verbs into *any* writing—on *any* topic? For example, suppose you are writing about whether television is a good or bad influence on viewers. Could you make strong verbs part of your response? Let's say you found a way to do that—and the writer next to you *only* used verbs like *is, are, was, were, have, has, be,* and *been*. Would that really make a big difference to the person reading the essays? Why?

Editing Level 1: Conventions

The Troublemakers

It's fare to say that **homophones**—words with similar pronunciations but vary different meanings—are knot for the feint of hart. Sum of them are reel troublemakers, giving anyone who reeds or rights fits. Sew what should wee dew with these troublemakers? Put them inn the corner? Give them a thyme out? Ground them four a weak? Hour suggestion is two take them on, you no, face yore fears and awl that. Yew get the point, write?

In this lesson, you are going to face some of the troublemakers, identify a few more to put on the list, and work to conquer them.

A Warm-Up

If you have ever used a spell-check program on a computer, then you know that computers (like many writers) struggle a bit with homophones. Therefore, if you rely on the spell-check program, you can spell everything correctly but still end up using the wrong words, as we did in the introduction. No big deal, right?

Actually—it *is.* That's because your meaning could be totally changed. To get a grip on homophones, you have to watch out for words that sound *just like* the one you want but are spelled differently and mean something else altogether. Here's a little warm-up with a few of the toughest homophones. (There are many more.) Read each sentence carefully, and then decide which of the homophone choices best completes the sentence.

1. Chuck's broken ankle could **lesson / lessen** his chances of making the track team.

2. If the **flu / flue/ flew** in the fireplace is blocked, smoke will back up and escape into the house.

3. As soon as he walked into his sister's room, Jorge sensed that his **presence / presents** wasn't welcome.

4. When you quote someone's words, be sure to **site/ cite / sight** the source.

5. The doctor's **patients / patience** was tested every time the twins came in for a check-up.

6. The **coarse / course** pepper left me sneezing violently.

7. I'm afraid I'm hooked on television **cereals / serials**.

Share and Compare

Compare your homophone choices with a partner's. Were these easy for you? Did you make the same choices? Use a dictionary to settle any disagreements.

The Troublemaker List

Following is a list of homophones for you to use as a reference. We suggest making a copy of this list for your writing notebook and adding to it as you encounter other homophones in your reading.

Homophones

adds, ads, adze

ade, aid, aide

aisle, I'll, isle

allowed, aloud

altar, alter

band, banned

bare, bear

board, bored

buy, by, bye

capital, capitol

ceiling, sealing

cell, sell

cellar, seller

cent, scent, sent

cereal, serial

chews, choose

cite, sight, site, (cited, sighted, sited)

close, clothes

coarse, course

colonel, kernel

cymbal, symbol

dew, do, due

die, dye, (died, dyed), (dies, dyes)

discussed, disgust

dual, duel

find, fined

flew, flu, flue

flour, flower

for, fore, four

forth, fourth

foul, fowl

frees, freeze

groan, grown

heal, heel

hear, here

heard, herd

hoarse, horse

hour, our

knight, night

knot, naught, not

know, no

lead, led

leased, least

lends, lens

lessen, lesson

loan, lone

mind, mined

miner, minor

pain, pane

pair, pare, pear

passed, past

patience, patients

pause, paws

peace, piece

poor, pore, pour

praise, prays, preys

presence, presents

principal, principle

racket, racquet

rain, reign, rein

raise, rays, raze

rap, wrap

read, reed

real, reel

recede, reseed

review, revue

role, roll

seam, seem

sighs, size

sole, soul

some, sum

suite, sweet

sundae, Sunday

tense, tents

their, there, they're

threw, through

tide, tied

verses, versus

waist, waste

wait, weight

ware, wear, where

yore, you're, your

The Top Six Troublemakers

As you read the list of homophones, you may have come across some personal troublemakers. Just knowing which words give you trouble as a writer puts you in a far better position to deal with them. Problem homophones may work themselves off the list as you conquer them—and you may wish to add others you encounter as a reader. List your own Top Six Troublemaker Homophones in the space below. This list is personal, so it won't look exactly like anyone else's.

My Personal Top Six Troublemaker Homophones

1. _____
2. _____
3. _____
4. _____
5. _____
6. _____

Editing Strategies

When you use homophones in your writing, what are three things you could do to make sure you choose the *right* word—not just the "right sounding" word?

1. _____
2. _____
3. _____

Let's put those strategies to work right now. Here are five more sentences to read and edit. This time, you don't have any choices to help you spot the homophones. You'll have to look for troublemakers yourself. Underline any homophone that you feel is the *right sounding* word but the *wrong* choice. Write the word with the correct spelling and meaning above the misused word.

1. I have to memorize all ten versus of this ancient poem, and it's a reel pain.

2. From my room, I could here my parents as they disgust whether or not I had worked hard enough to deserve a new tennis racket.

3. If my brother lens his camera to his friend, it could come back with sum miner damage.

4. I herd that the principle was going too honor a pare of students for they're charity work.

5. For our research project, we have to correctly site any Web cites we use, and that always seams to be hard fore me.

I found ____ homophone errors.

Quiz Maker

Look over the homophone list carefully until you come to a set you think might stump someone from your writing circle. Then create your own quiz on a clean sheet of scratch paper. Use our seven Warm-Up sentences as models. Write one sentence using one set of homophones. Set up your sentence so that your teammate must make a choice from two or three possible words—just as we did in the Warm-Up. In your writing circles, trade quizzes and discuss the results. Be sure you know the answer so you can explain it!

A Writer's Questions
Why is writing quiz questions one of the best ways to learn something yourself? Do you think this helps teachers learn and remember?

Editing Level 2: Presentation
Today's Specials

What's on the menu for *you* today? Menus—*that's* what! Menu writing is all about clear, descriptive word choice and enticing presentation. After all, menu writers are trying to persuade customers to order something—the more the better. Customers, in turn, are looking for the information they need to make good choices. Vegetarians want to know if a dish contains meat. Pizza lovers want to know how many toppings they can pick from. A fish lover might be hungry for salmon—but only if it is grilled. And that person who can never make up his or her mind (you know who we mean) will look carefully at the wording and illustrations for every single item. Whether a menu comes on a single sheet of paper, bound in a leather book, or is handwritten on a chalkboard, the wording and presentation determine what—if anything—customers will order.

A Warm-Up

Maybe you are an experienced menu reader—you've seen everything from pizza take-out menus to fancy sit-down menus with daily specials sheets. Or maybe you've only dined out a few times. Either way, you probably know what to expect from a menu. Before looking at some example menus, take a moment and create a list on the following page of some things you'd expect to find on any menu—from wording to layout, what do most menus have in common?

Menu Details

1. _____
2. _____
3. _____
4. _____
5. _____
6. _____

Exploring . . . and Making notes

Now, with the guidance of your teacher, spend a few minutes exploring various kinds of menus—from elegant restaurants, diners or cafes, chains, fast food restaurants, local favorites, and so on.

As you explore, notice where your eyes are drawn. Which items make you so hungry you want to eat *right now?* Do any descriptions tempt you to try something you've never eaten before? Make some notes about effective wording, organization, design, colors, pictures, and so on. Write your notes here:

My Notes on Menus

_____
_____
_____
_____
_____
_____
_____

Presentation Practice

You, the Critic

Following are several menu items from a new restaurant, House of Food, that is planning a big opening in a just a few weeks. (Sorry, we made this one up.) As a menu critic, you have been asked to do a critique of this menu. On your own paper or in the space below, make notes to the restaurant owners. Be specific with your comments. Your goal is to help them fine-tune their menu, not make them feel bad. Consider such things as:

- Choice of fonts
- Illustrations
- Wording in the descriptions of items
- Layout on the page (Attractive? Appealing?)
- Organization of information (Is it easy to find what you want?)

HINT: Menu descriptions are meant to be both helpful and persuasive. Feel free to make specific word choice and presentation suggestions. Ready? Bon appétit!

House of Food
A Place to Eat

The Big Burger $3.21

It's a really big burger on a pretty big bun without all the yucky stuff you hate. With your choice of toppings.

Ham and Cheese Omelet $6.54

A fluffy, three-egg omelet loaded with diced Virginia ham and Wisconsin sharp cheddar. Served with oven roasted red potatoes and your choice of homemade buttermilk biscuit, sourdough, whole wheat, seven-grain, or honey-oat toast.

House of Food Special Platter of Food $9.87

This one will bust your gut before it busts your wallet. Piled high!

Steaming hot! Side of butter!

Your choice of a tub of brown or white gravy.

THE DEEP END OF THE FRYER $11.10

If you like your, well, everything deep-fried, then this dish is for you. There are no choices to make—you get it all! Deep-fried catfish, ling cod, shrimp, chicken, octopus, noodles, chili, mozzarella sticks, bean burrito, okra, green beans, pickles, shoestring potatoes, hush puppies, with a side of deep-fried butter, all Served on a 24-inch platter (platter not deep-fried)

Dessert suggestion: Deep-fried ice cream with deep-fried chocolate cookies.

Share and Compare

Take a few moments to share your notes with another group or with the whole class. Be sure to talk about anything this menu designer did well—along with your suggestions for improvement. Is there any item you would order?

A Writer's Questions

Is it possible to over-describe an item on a menu? What's the problem for the reader if a menu is too detailed? Do menu writers tend to give you more information than you want about some things—and not enough about others? Is this true for all types of writing?

Presentation Matters

For this last part of the lesson, you'll work in a writing circle to create a menu for a hypothetical restaurant. You can work on everything together or divide the tasks in any way you wish. If you have access, you may do all of your work on a computer. If not, create your menu by hand. Here are some things to keep in mind:

- Name your restaurant, and be as original as possible. (Remember, the name might want to give a hint about the kind of food you serve.)

- Name and describe at least five menu items—salads, breakfast items, sandwiches, pizzas, desserts—whatever you love to eat or make.

- Make your word choice clear, but not overdone. Remember to appeal to the senses. How does the food look? Sound as it's cooking? Smell? Taste? Feel on the tongue?

- Remember that menu descriptions are persuasive writing, mini-ads trying to sell each dish.

- Choose fonts and graphics to complement your descriptions and help customers make good choices.

- Decide if your menu will be a single sheet, single-fold, tri-fold, or your own layout idea.

Sample Paper 15

Score for Word Choice _____

Invaders of Our Land

About a century ago, some predacious scholar who consumed a voracious amount of Shakespeare got the atrocious idea to import to America all of the birds indigenous to Shakespeare's plays. Among his ultimate selections was the very precocious starling, a vile bird that has since wreaked all sorts of precipitant mischief upon the prosperous American landscape.

Among the birds' less tolerant traits is its inveterate habit of taking over the gullible nests of other bird species. There, once established, it incorporates its own eggs, leaving the unsuspecting mother bird to raise the fledgling starlings as her own. Nor does the hostile starling's harsh devastation end there. Starlings consume prodigious amounts of various and lucrative grains, leaving deflated livestock without native resources and frustrated farmers without incremental income.

All in all, the importation of animals and flora to areas where they do not propagate may seem a wise venture, but it is definitely one that terminates in regret.

Sources

1999. Feare, Chris. *Starlings and Mynas*. Princeton, NJ: Princeton University Press.

Roger Tory Peterson. *Peterson Field Guide to Birds of North America*. New York, NY: Houghton Mifflin Company, 2009.

Sample Paper 16
Score for Word Choice _____

To the Bat House!

If you're having problems with comic book criminals like the Joker, then the crime fighting superhero Batman is just the guy you need to save the day. Light up the Gotham City sky with the Bat Signal, and he'll appear. But what if you don't happen to live in Gotham? Let's say you have a backyard insect problem, like hordes of buzzing mosquitoes keeping you penned up in your house every night of the summer. Batman is not the answer, but real bats *are*. You won't need the Bat Signal to attract them—they probably wouldn't respond anyway. What *will* get their attention is a specially designed bat house.

The idea of attracting bats *on purpose* makes a lot of people downright nervous. Bats are dirty, like rats with wings, right? Wrong! Bats are actually very clean mammals, like humans or dogs. Hold on a minute, though. Even if they're immaculate, they'll *still* suck your blood and give you rabies, right? Wrong! Only three out of over 1,000 bat species are vampire bats, and they live in Central and South America or in Mexico. Less than one percent of bats even *have* rabies and those that do rarely transmit the disease to humans. Are you warming to the idea of having bats move into your back yard? Well, before you decide, just realize that you haven't even heard the best part yet.

Remember the hypothetical mosquito problem? By welcoming bats to your yard with a bat house (you'll find hundreds of easy designs online, by the way), you are solving your buzzing bug problem without a single dangerous chemical. Bats are capable of consuming up to 1,000 mosquitoes in an hour and about half their body weight in bugs each night. They're more efficient than tiny, self-propelled vacuums, and unlike vacuums, they're silent. You won't hear them coming—and neither will the insects.

What's more, bats are very undemanding. All they need is a water supply and a place to rest after each insect feast. The best part is that it's all *natural* pest control—no noisy zappers or poisonous pesticides. Your garden, if you have one, can now be chemical free! Oh—and in case you were wondering, they will *not* dive bomb you as you stroll through the back yard, or attempt to nest in your hair. Those too are myths. Bats only target what they eat—and that does not include humans. Their aim is incredibly precise (a bat can easily nail a mosquito that's twenty yards away), so they don't bump into things as large as humans by accident.

By building a bat house you are maintaining balance in your yard's ecosystem while saving the money you would have spent on toxic products to kill insects. You are also helping others to understand and appreciate bats rather than fear them. Bats have been eating insects for thousands of years. That's an impressive resume. Why not put all that experience to work for you?

Sources

Brown, Carla. "Build a Bat House." *Garden For Wildlife*. National Wildlife Federation. 16 Oct. 2009 <http://www.nwf.org/gardenforwildlife/bathouse.cfm>.

Hutson, Tony. *Bats*. Stillwater, MN: Voyageur Press, 2000.

"The Importance of Bat Houses." *Organization for Bat Conservation*. 16 Oct. 2009 <http://www.batconservation.org/content/Bathouseimportance.html>.

Tuttle, Merlin D. *The Bat House Builder's Handbook*. Austin, TX: Bat Conservation International, 2005.

"Welcome." *Houses for Bats*. AML Enterprises. 17 Oct. 2009 <http://www.housesforbats.com/>.

Name _____ Date _____

Revising Checklist for Word Choice

☐ I found some strong words or phrases to highlight. AND . . .

☐ I <u>underlined</u> words and phrases I need to revise.

☐ I found my OWN way to say things. I avoided tired, overused expressions.

☐ _____ rated my writing for Word Choice:

1	2	3	4	5	6

☐ Three verbs that really work in my writing: _____, _____, and _____.

☐ I used sensory details to help readers experience _____ sights, _____ sounds, _____ feelings, _____ smells, _____ tastes.

☐ I crossed out clutter (words I did not need).

☐ I know the meaning of *every word I used.* OR, I need to look these words up:
_____, _____, _____.

☐ I replaced ALL general words like *nice, good, great,* or *wonderful* with specific, descriptive words that show an insider's understanding of this topic.

☐ If I used any NEW words, I made sure the meaning was clear.

☐ I spelled my words correctly so readers would know which words I meant.

> **Note** The words you choose make a bridge of meaning from you to your reader. Did you take time to make the BEST choices you could? Would readers learn any new words from your writing—or is there a phrase or two that might linger in their minds?

Sentence Fluency

Have you ever taken a car ride with a driver who seems to have one foot on the accelerator and one foot on the brake at all times? Zoom! STOP! Z-o-o-o-o-m! STOP! Instead of enjoying the ride, you are bracing yourself for the next shift in speed. If you write as if you have one foot on the accelerator and one foot on the brake, your readers will be bracing themselves, too. Smooth writing—what many writers call **fluency**—is easier to achieve when you think of your readers' comfort as they navigate their way through the text.

Many writing strategies can improve Sentence Fluency. In this unit, you'll practice

- combining short, choppy sentences.
- varying sentence length and structure.
- using transition words effectively—and in moderation.
- combining multiple strategies to make a passage fluent.

Sample Paper 17

Score for Sentence Fluency _____

This Won't Hurt a Bit

When was the last time you had a to have an injection? Yes, a shot—like in the arm, backside, leg, or mouth. Do you remember it? Chances are you do. For some people, it's downright traumatic. What's more, just before you flinched, cried, or passed out, you probably heard someone utter the famous line, "Relax! This won't hurt a bit." Then, of course, the old needle poked you. Ouch!

Now there may be an alternative to a poke in the arm—or at least one is being tested and developed. Chemists and doctors in Oxford, England have discovered a way to make injections virtually pain-free. The secret is a space-age tube that injects drugs under the skin at supersonic speeds, using helium, of all things. (And no, floating weightless like a balloon is not one of the side effects, though some people might like that so much they wouldn't even care about pain anymore.)

With this type of injection, the drug particles are extremely tiny, so when they penetrate, the patient feels almost nothing. That's worth repeating: *almost nothing.* Better still, doctors who have tried the new supersonic tube claim they can measure dosages with much greater accuracy than was possible using the old syringe method. This makes injections not only painless, but much safer in the bargain.

Of course, no one has said for sure whether the dose of helium raises the pitch of the patient's voice. In the future, we may hear tiny, mouse-like voices joyously squeaking, "Thanks! That didn't hurt a bit!"

Sample Paper 18
Score for Sentence Fluency _____

Teaching Dad to Ski

We bought my dad skis for his birthday. We had to teach him how. He has lived his whole life near the mountains. He never learned to ski, though. We spent one whole day on the slopes with him. We could see why.

He had trouble even putting on his skis, which is easy. He couldn't master it. He just kept getting angry and impatient. He was cursing the skis and the people who make them. He told us to just go on ahead and leave him. He would catch up when he finally got his blankety-blank skis on.

My dad didn't get his skis on until lunchtime. We got him to try one small hill. It had hardly any slope to it. He acted like it was Mt. Everest. He barely got moving. We told him to bend his knees. He kept looking at us and yelling back. We probably distracted him. He went into a snowdrift!

He was stuck in the snowdrift and he was swinging his poles. We could see them sticking out over the snow. He would swing his poles and then slam them in the snow. He finally got out. He sat down on the back of his skis. He went down the whole hill that way. We laughed so hard we fell over. He never heard us. He was yelling too loud. He would not go down the hill a second time. He said it was definitely time for lunch.

Sentence Fluency

The WRITER...
creates smooth, rhythmic, fluid sentences.

So the READER...
_____
_____
_____

The WRITER...
uses variety or purposeful repetition.

So the READER...
_____
_____
_____

The WRITER...
creates long and short sentences—even occasional fragments.

So the READER...
_____
_____
_____

The WRITER...
begins each sentence in a meaningful way.

So the READER...
_____
_____
_____

Keeping It Rolling

How much fun would longboarding, inline skating, or bike riding be if you had to stop and restart every five feet? Good writing needs to keep rolling along, too. Periods should signal a smooth, gradual stop—not a slam-on-the-brakes interruption. To find out whether you're giving your readers a smooth ride, read your writing aloud, every word and sentence. If it doesn't flow well for you, it's time to revise.

Sharing an Example: The Rules of the Game

Quietly read aloud the following passage. As you read, ask yourself, *Does this passage roll along smoothly? Is it easy to read with natural expression?* If your answer is no to either question, take another close look to figure out why.

The Rules of the Game

I think there's no better sport than ice hockey. Ice hockey is the King of Sports for me. Hockey is an exciting game. It's exciting because of the speed. The players move fast. The puck moves fast. It's also exciting because of the physical contact. That contact is called checking.

Some of the rules make it exciting, too. The referees are right on the ice. The referee's job is to enforce the rules. Players get a penalty for breaking a rule. Players who break rules have to sit in the penalty box. They may have to sit in the penalty box for two minutes or more. This gives the other team an extra player advantage on the ice. That advantage is called a "power play." Power plays often lead to goals.

Hockey is a great game. It's a really great game to watch live. It's an even better game when you understand the rules.

Respond

As a *reader*, how would you rate the fluency of this passage from **1** (about as smooth as square wheels on a gravel road) to **6** (like a hockey puck sliding over ice):

| 1 | 2 | 3 | 4 | 5 | 6 | 7 | 8 | 9 | 10 |

Analyze

What specific strengths or problems with fluency did you notice in "The Rules of the Game"? Work with a partner or in a writing circle to make a list of things you notice. (You may look at a checklist or rubric as you work—but trust your own responses, too!)

1. _____

2. _____

3. _____

4. _____

5. _____

Share and Compare

Share your thoughts with the class as a whole and work with
your teacher to make a list of strengths and problems.

The Rules of the Game, Draft 2

No matter how you rated "The Rules of the Game" for
fluency, chances are you have some ideas on how it could
be improved. (So do we, and we'll share them in a bit.) With
a partner or in a writing circle, create a new draft. We left
room on the page for you to revise, but you can write on
scratch paper if that's easier. As you work, feel free to

- combine sentences.
- cross out words.
- add details.
- change wording to smooth the flow.
- do anything to make the piece read smoothly.

Reflect

The original draft has 20 sentences. Count the sentences
in your revision. How does it compare? What does this
tell you about the original—and about the revision strategy
you used?

Have someone who has not seen your draft read it aloud and
then rate it, **1** to **10,** from his or her perspective as a reader.
Mark that person's score here:

| 1 | 2 | 3 | 4 | 5 | 6 | 7 | 8 | 9 | 10 |

Combining Sentences = Combining Ideas

Did you use sentence combining as one of your strategies? (We did.) When you combine sentences, you're actually putting several ideas together in one concise sentence. You are also decreasing the total number of words. To see how sentence combining works, look at these four sentences from "The Rules of the Game." We have underlined the key idea in each sentence to show how four little ideas can easily be grouped together in one smooth sentence.

Players <u>can get a penalty.</u>

+ They get a penalty <u>for breaking a rule.</u>

+ Players who break rules <u>have to sit in the penalty box.</u>

+ Players may have to sit <u>for two minutes or more.</u>

= **A player who gets a penalty for breaking a rule must sit in the penalty box for two minutes or more.**

From 34 words to 21! No more stop and go—and that makes for one smooth ride.

A Combination Warm-Up

Using the previous example as a warm-up, combine the following four choppy sentences into one longer, smoother sentence. Begin by identifying and underlining the key ideas in each of the four choppy sentences. Then try putting ALL those bits of information together in one long, flowing sentence.

Deer pose problems for gardeners.

+ They pose a problem because they eat plants.

+ Deer will eat almost any kind of plant.

+ Deer are extremely hard to discourage.

= _____

_____

Get This Writing Rolling!

After that exercise, you are likely ready for some major combining work. Read the following passage carefully—more than once. The second time through, put a plus sign (+) between sentences you think could go together. Then revise with some careful combining. Draw a line through words you no longer need and insert new words to smooth the flow.

May Flower Service Project

My school has a tradition. The tradition we have is delivering flowers on May 1. We deliver the flowers to people in the neighborhood. The neighborhood is around our school. We don't knock or ring doorbells. We leave the flowers on people's porches. There is a note attached to the flowers. The note says "Happy May Day from your friends at Whitford Middle School." The flowers we leave are for planting. The flowers could be planted in flowerbeds or a garden. Some of the neighbors write notes. They send the notes to the school. The notes say how much they appreciate the flowers. The notes reinforce the importance of the project. They are only little flowers, but they can really brighten someone's day.

Name _____   Date _____

Share and Compare

Meet with a partner or in a writing circle to share revisions. Take turns reading aloud, listening for the smooth flow. You may also wish to compare numbers of sentences in your final copies. The original had 15 sentences—a lot more than were needed. How many sentences does your revision have? Do any of your revisions improve the flow of the original draft? Discuss your improvements.

A Writer's Questions

A skillful writer could probably just keep combining and combining, ultimately turning a long string of short sentences into a short string of *long* sentences. But—is that really the goal in sentence combining? And if not, what *is* the goal?

Putting It to the Test

Writers working under pressure may resort to a simplistic method of combining sentences—just linking ideas together with the conjunction *and*. Unfortunately, this sometimes transforms choppy sentences into a run-on sentence. What other combining strategies could you suggest for a writer working under pressure?

Tuning In to Variety

Variety doesn't work with everything. If some hours ran 60 minutes while others ran 47.5 minutes, our days would be difficult to organize. Writing, however, thrives on variety, especially when it comes to sentence length and structure. Too much unintentional repetition creates a monotonous rhythm that makes readers tune out. Variety wakes readers up like a new song on the radio. In this lesson, you will practice varying sentence length in order to keep readers tuned in to your message.

Sharing an Example: *The Time Machine*

In the following passage, the time traveler buckles into his machine and embarks on his first leap into the future. Read the passage aloud, paying particular attention to the sentence fluency. Then read it once more, noticing sentence lengths and beginnings.

I took the starting lever in one hand and the stopping one in the other, pressed the first, and almost immediately the second. I seemed to reel. I felt a nightmare sensation of falling; and, looking round, I saw the laboratory exactly as before. Had anything happened? Then I noted the clock. A moment before it had stood at a minute or so past ten. Now it was nearly half-past three!

I drew a breath, set my teeth, gripped the starting lever with both hands, and went off with a thud. The night came like the turning out of a lamp, and in another moment came tomorrow. The laboratory grew faint and hazy, then fainter and ever fainter.

Name   Date

Tomorrow night came black, then day again, night again, day again, faster and faster still.

The Time Machine
by H.G. Wells

Respond

From your perspective as a reader, rate the fluency of this passage from **1** (repetitive and hard to read) to **10** (highly varied and easy to read):

1	2	3	4	5	6	7	8	9	10

What Else Did You Notice?

Without looking back, make your best guess about each of the following:

- How many sentences begin in different ways?
  ☐ all   ☐ most   ☐ very few
- How many words are in the shortest sentence? _____
- How many words are in the longest sentence? _____
- What is the writer writing about *mainly?* _____
  _____
- Is there a topic sentence in this passage? _____

Share and Compare

Compare your responses with a partner or in a writing circle. Also compare your ratings (**1** to **10**). Then, with the class, review the passage and discuss the variety and fluency.

Analyze to Revise

Here's another passage to analyze. Read it aloud, softly, to yourself. As you read, ask yourself, *Is this easy to read? How fluent is it? What could make it stronger?*

Prisoner of the Food Channel

I think I could be a neglected child. I think I am technology-neglected. I think my parents are technology-challenged. We have only one computer. We have no electronic games. We have only one TV in our house. We keep it in the family room. We don't even have a flat screen. I don't have a TV in my room. My friends all have TVs in their rooms. My parents think TV time should be family time. We might as well live back in the 1950s. We need to come into the 21st Century. I would like one TV just for me. I could watch things I like. I would not have to watch cooking shows. Anything is better than the Food Channel.

Respond

Rate the fluency of the TV passage from **1** (repetitive and choppy) to **10** (highly varied and readable—a gem of fluency):

| 1 | 2 | 3 | 4 | 5 | 6 | 7 | 8 | 9 | 10 |

What Else Did You Notice?

Answer the following questions without looking back at the Food Channel piece. When you've answered them, go back to see if your first impressions were right.

- How many sentences begin in different ways?
  - ☐ Every single one—the variety was amazing!
  - ☐ Most—the only repetition was for special effect.
  - ☐ Very few—the repetition got tiresome.

Name _____   Date _____

- About how many words were in the shortest sentence? _____
- About how many words were in the longest sentence? _____
- What is this writer writing about *mainly?* _____

  _____

  _____

- Is there a topic sentence? _____

Share and Compare

Compare your responses with a partner or in a writing circle. Also compare your ratings (**1** to **10**). Then, discuss the fluency of this passage as a class.

Make a Plan

With your partner or in a writing circle, make a plan for revising "Prisoner of the Food Channel." What are the main strategies you need to apply to make this piece fluent? Jot down three or four ideas.

1. _____

2. _____

3. _____

4. _____

Putting Your Strategies to Work

Work together on a revision of "Prisoner of the Food Channel," putting your strategies to work. Remember to quietly read aloud to yourself as you go. Your goal is to make the passage as fluent and readable as possible. Imagine someone reading it for the very first time with ease.

Name _____ Date _____

_____
_____
_____
_____
_____
_____
_____
_____
_____
_____
_____
_____
_____
_____
_____
_____
_____
_____
_____
_____
_____
_____

Share and Compare

Share your revision of "Prisoner of the Food Channel" with another group or the whole class. Discuss the strategies you used to bring out the fluency. Did your revisions also influence the voice of the piece?

Writing with Fluency

Choosing a Topic

Revising the work of others can influence the way you write as you draft. Try it and see. First, choose a topic from our list or—better yet—come up with your own. Pick something you can write on quickly and easily, something about which you have a lot to say. We kept our topics broad so you can narrow them to suit yourself:

- The unfairness of it all
- It turned out to be a myth
- A true legend
- I remember it well . . . OR
- My own idea: _____

Planning and Drafting

Once you have your topic clearly in mind, take about 5 minutes to plan your writing. Make a sketch or idea web, list some questions you plan to answer, list details you want to remember, or do any kind of planning that works for you. With a plan at your side, write steadily for 15 minutes or more. Keep the ideas flowing—and go for variety. Be daring. Start some sentences in ways you never tried before.

Share and Compare

Share your draft with your partner or writing circle. Read aloud with expression, and let your teammates know what you'd like them to listen for. As a listener, pay close attention to fluency and comment on the variety you hear.

Name _____   Date _____

A Writer's Questions

In this lesson, you focused on revising a draft for fluency. By doing this, did you also strengthen other traits—ideas, voice, or word choice, for example? What does this tell you about the process of revision?

Putting It to the Test

In on-demand writing, writers are not always given true revision time. Often, *revision* means simply reading over a draft and correcting obvious errors, such as misspelled or missing words. If you found yourself in such a situation and you wanted to be sure to weave some sentence variety into your writing, what could you do to make this happen?

Avoiding Transition Overload!

All of us overeat occasionally. Remember that time you ate seven slices of pizza instead of the usual three? (Or maybe that was one of us as we were writing and editing this unit late one night!) Anyway, anything can be overdone, not just pizza. Take transitions, which are words or phrases like *next, therefore, in addition, moreover,* and *in other words.* Used well, transitions keep your ideas clear and connected. But too much of a good thing, like that seventh slice of pizza, can make a reader feel on overload.

Sharing an Example: The Monkey's Paw

Following is a slightly revised passage from "The Monkey's Paw" by W.W. Jacobs. With apologies to Mr. Jacobs, we have piled on a few extra transitional words and phrases. See if you can identify the transitions we added—the ones the author never put in. Then go ahead and cross them out.

First of all, the talisman was in its place, and, moreover, a horrible fear that the unspoken wish might bring his mutilated son before him ere he could escape from the room seized upon him. In addition, his brow cold with sweat, he felt his way round the table, and as a result groped along the wall until he found himself in the small passage with the unwholesome thing in his hand.

After that, even his wife's face seemed changed as he entered the room. But all the same, it was white and expectant, and in fact his fears seemed to have an unnatural look upon it. In conclusion, he was afraid of her.

"*Wish!*" she cried, in a strong voice.

"It is foolish and wicked," he faltered.

"*Wish!*" repeated his wife.

He raised his hand. "I wish my son alive again."

Your Response

How did this passage sound and feel to you? Was it on transition overload—or did you find very few words to cross out?

☐ This passage was as smooth as a boat gliding through water. I didn't cross out one word.

☐ I crossed out a *few* words, but most of the transitions were needed.

☐ I crossed out one word after another. Transition overload was weighing the writing down like rocks!

Listen and Reflect

Listen to your teacher read the original version of "The Monkey's Paw" aloud as you follow along. Silently reread the text of our revised version as you listen. Then discuss the difference between the two versions. Which transitions are in the original? Which one—with or without transitions added—is more fluent to your ear? Why?

Overloaded—Or Not?

Read the following piece aloud with a pen or pencil in hand. Ask yourself, *Which transitions are* helpful *in creating fluency and meaning, and which ones get in the way?* Cross out any transitional words or phrases you think are unneeded or more confusing than helpful.

First of all, I don't remember the exact time of the accident, but I do, however, in fact, remember the collision of the two shuttle vans. To repeat, although I didn't look at my watch for instance, I did nevertheless see the moment of impact between the two vehicles. Before we could shuttle to town, however, first we had to pick up our checked luggage and, second, immediately call the hotel, moreover, to send the courtesy van over. Meanwhile, the courtesy van was late on top of everything else. As a result, we were all on the lookout for it. Finally, it arrived. As soon as the driver began to open his door, however, another shuttle vehicle pulled along side and nevertheless slammed into the hotel van's door of all things. In conclusion, on the other hand, it was a pretty nerve-racking way to begin our trip.

© Great Source. Permission is granted to copy this page.

Name _____   Date _____

Share and Compare

Meet with a partner to share your work. Take turns reading your revisions aloud—and discuss the changes you made. Was this piece on transition overload? Did your revision make the meaning clearer—and help readers focus on the message?

Transitions in Moderation

Whereas seven slices of pizza might be too many for most of us, half a slice might not be enough. Most things—including pizza and transitions—work best in moderation. How moderate are *you* in using transitions?

We have chosen some writing topics that we think will lead you naturally into the use of transitional words. However, feel free to choose your own topic if you prefer. Take about 5 minutes to plan and another 15 to write, using transitions in moderation. Suggested topics:

- Compare two kinds of pets
- Compare elementary and middle school experiences
- Explain step by step how to make pizza—or do any simple task
- Create a persuasive argument for or against cell phone use in cars
- Create a quick summary of the highlights (good and bad) of the last year . . . OR
- Create a topic of your choice: _____

_____

Sentence Fluency ⟳

Name .... Date ....

Share and Compare

Meet with a partner or in a writing circle to share your drafts. Look and listen for transitional words and expressions in your own writing—and that of your classmates. Did you all achieve a good balance? Was anyone on transition overload? Did any of you *omit* transitions that would have been helpful? Take this opportunity to make some light revisions.

A Writer's Questions
Achieving balance—in anything—can be tricky. As a writer, how do you know when you've achieved the right balance with your transitions—enough to connect ideas clearly but not so many that you will overwhelm your readers?

Putting It to the Test
Could there be a reason that transitions are particularly important in on-demand writing? What do transitional words and phrases tell you, as a reader, about the writer's train of thought? Why is that so important in a testing situation?

Putting It All Together

Suppose, at the very beginning of this unit, someone had handed you a two-page manuscript and said, "Here. Revise this for fluency." Would you have known what to do? If so, good for you! If not, maybe you have a few more ideas up your reviser's sleeve now. We hope so, because revision—really good, purposeful revision—depends on skills. Can you recall the skills you practiced in the last three lessons? Brainstorm a quick class list. Then your teacher will offer you some reminders.

Choosing a Good Topic

This lesson begins with the creation of a writing sample. And as you know, that begins with choosing a topic. This time, however, choosing has two parts, and you'll work with your writing circle for both of them.

Part 1

We have a hunch you'll like this part. You get to coach your teacher in coming up with a writing topic he or she likes. Have a 5-minute discussion. Think about a topic you feel would be right because (1) it's something your teacher knows a lot

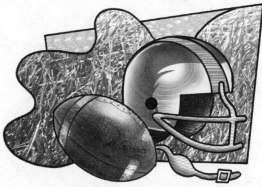

about or definitely finds interesting and (2) it's a topic you would enjoy reading about. At the end of the 5 minutes, be prepared to offer 1 or 2 suggestions—no more. Your teacher will make a choice after hearing all suggestions (but may or may not share that choice with you just yet).

Part 2

You're probably not surprised to discover that it's now *your* turn to come up with a topic. We're not offering any hints or lists this time. You're on your own—except that you have the help of your writing circle teammates. Take about 6 to 8 minutes to think of a good writing topic. Choose something you know well—and something you think YOUR TEAM will enjoy reading about. **HINT:** You can all write about the same general topic, but each person can approach it in his or her own way.

Writing a Draft

For this part of the lesson, you will work on your own. Take about 5 minutes to do some planning, using any prewriting strategy you like: reading and thinking, sketching, making a list or web, etc. Then write for about 15 minutes. As you write, be sure you

- write on every other line to allow room for revision.
- leave big margins.
- keep your main message clearly in mind.
- read along in your head as you write, as if you were reading aloud.

Name _____ Date _____

Sharing, Listening, Responding

Part 1

Listen as your teacher shares his or her draft aloud. Be prepared to offer honest, helpful, supportive feedback. Comment on the strengths you hear as well as any strategies you feel he or she could use to improve as a writer.

Part 2

Now read your own work in your writing group, keeping in mind your role as a responder and writer.

As a Responder . . . Ask writers questions or offer suggestions about strategies to improve fluency. Be sure every comment supports your classmate as a writer.

As a Writer . . . When it's your time to share, listen with an open mind to your group's feedback. Make notes to remember helpful suggestions. Be prepared to put the most useful suggestions into action. Good feedback is all about improving your writing!

Reflecting . . .

Now that you've shared and discussed your writing sample, you're ready to revise—almost. Before you start, take a moment to reflect on specific strategies you think will be helpful. Think about the comments from your group and your own response to your draft. Put a check next to each of the revision strategies you think could make your writing stronger.

☐ **Combine choppy sentences** to create longer, more rhythmic ones.

☐ **Vary sentence length.**

☐ **Shorten sentences** that are too long.

☐ **Select strong, appropriate transitional words** to connect ideas.

☐ **Eliminate transition overload.**

☐ **Vary sentence beginnings** to avoid monotonous repetition.

. . . Then Revising

Revise your draft for the trait of Fluency. Go back frequently to read it aloud, getting the feel and the sound. Think about

- Variety
- Rhythm
- Meaning
- Readability

Take your time. Go back more than once. Be a bit ruthless. Imagine your draft was written by someone else—someone who said, "Give me all the help you can!" Put your heart, soul, and pencil into it.

Share and Compare

Regroup in your writing circles. This time, before you read your draft, tell which feedback helped you most and why. Explain *how* you revised. Then read your revision. As others share their revisions, think about additional strategies—or sentence styles—you could try next time.

A Writer's Questions

Suppose that as a writer—and you're getting to be an experienced writer, after all—you disagree with the feedback you receive from a partner or writing group. What should you do? Follow it anyway? Discuss your options. Do reviewers always know best?

Putting It to the Test

Right now, if you wanted to, you could reach for a rubric and score the writing you just finished for fluency—or for any trait. (And you might even want to do that.) Let's say you were taking a writing test, though, and you didn't have a rubric handy. Could you still assess your own writing pretty effectively? How?

Rev-edit-ising, Anyone?

OK, *rev-edit-ising* is a bit of a mouthful, but you know how we came up with this new term? Yes, by combining *revising* and *editing*. We usually think of revision as coming before editing. Why edit what you might delete, right? However, when there are numerous errors, clearing away problems with spelling, punctuation, and grammar can make it easier to spot bigger problems, such as rough or awkward sentences that could use some smoothing out. It's a little like cleaning your room by first picking up the debris, then discovering a stain on the carpet. Debris—whether in your room or in a piece of writing—can keep other problems hidden.

A Warm-Up

For this practice, you'll edit first. Just focus on mistakes. Do you have your editor's tools ready—copyeditor symbols, dictionary, and a good writing handbook? A well-sharpened favorite pencil will help, too.

Here's a quick list of things to check. It's a list that every professional editor in every kind of industry uses! Review this checklist to make sure you don't miss anything. Read each of the two samples twice, once for meaning and once with pencil in hand to edit. Take about 3 minutes for each sample.

Editor's Checklist

- ✏ Spelling
- ✏ Capital letters
- ✏ Ending punctuation
- ✏ Internal punctuation—commas, quotation marks, etc.
- ✏ Grammar (subject-verb agreement, etc.)
- ✏ Missing or repeated words

Example A

their are a lot of people living in america who can't find the united states on a map of the world it's hard to believe isn't it imagine if the same people were asked to find Tunisia Americans need to become more aware of rest of the world around them

Example B

if someone ever comes up to you on the street or in the classroom and asks if you could find tunisia on a world map, would you no where to look here are some hints its in northern africa its on the mediterranean see its in between algeria and libia capital tunis

Share and Compare

Compare your edits and revisions with a partner's. Did you both make the same corrections? As you share and compare, be sure to mark any changes you missed. Then coach your teacher as he or she edits and revises each piece.

When you finish, go back and quietly read aloud your clean copy. Make any revisions you need to smooth the sentence flow. **HINT:** Don't be afraid to "test read" a sentence several different ways in your head. Professional writers often talk out loud as they work.

Shifting into Overdrive

By now you should be warmed up and ready for a tougher super-editor challenge. Here's a piece from a writer who has left a lot of editing and revising to be done. (We know you would never do this to yourself!) The task is challenging but not impossible. It just requires some patience. Follow these steps:

1. Read the passage aloud to get a sense of its message.

2. Read again, pencil in hand, to edit.

3. Use the Editor's Checklist to make sure you don't miss anything.

4. Read the piece a third time to smooth out the sentences.

A New Motto

Whenever my parents think that im demanding something instead of asking politely one of them always says you can't expect to both grand and comfortable its this saying that we found engraved on brass plate and stuck on the bricks just above the fireplace in in the house we moved into three year ago im not even sure what it meansmy dad tried to explain something about having to work some of the extras in life I remembered him that I'm only thirteen adolescence is tough I made a huge mistake I told him that none of my friends have to live according to wacky sayings engraved on brass plates he ghot going about how he and my mom don't care what my friends have or what rules they choose to live by ive heard this speech two millions time before I guess ive just got to start acting the way they want me until I can get my own motto stuck on the fireplace whatever the kid wants the kid gets

Share and Compare

Compare your work with your partner's. Start with editing. Did you find and correct the same errors?

Then compare revisions by having your partner read your final copy aloud. Did you change sentences in similar ways? How much rewriting did you do? Was one of you a little more daring in experimenting with the sentence flow?

A Writer's Questions

Think about revising and editing your own work. What do you like to do first—revise or edit? Or do you tend to weave them together? Do you think there's a "best" way to go about this—or do writers shift their strategy as they become more skilled?

Editing Level 2: Presentation

Concrete Poetry

Do you like poetry? Before you answer, remember that not all poetry has to be old, rhyme, or be about love. Here's a brand of poetry that seems to break all the rules, and even if you aren't a big fan of most poetry, maybe you'll like this kind. *Concrete poetry,* sometimes known as shape or visual poetry, depends on the use of good, heavy, thick cement. We're kidding. Actually, it depends on *presentation*—how words are placed and spaced on the page. The layout is as important as the message. In fact, the layout IS part of the message. Concrete poems bend and twist fonts and sentences to create visual images that make readers smile—or see things in a different way.

A Warm-Up

You've probably heard someone read or recite poetry. Maybe you've even attended a poetry slam or participated in some kind of poetry competition. Concrete poems wouldn't work well in these situations because just hearing one doesn't give listeners the whole message. However, concrete poems would do very well in an art gallery because it's the *art of the poem*—presentation and text working together—that delivers the poet's message.

Look through some poetry books that your teacher has assembled or find examples of concrete poetry online. Take your time. Notice the layout of each poem, paying particular attention to the way everything works together to guide your eye and gradually reveal the full meaning.

When you finish browsing, check out these three examples of concrete poems. Review them with a partner or in a writing circle. Talk about what you like and why the poet chose a particular design. Do you have a favorite? Also, share any favorites you discovered through your own exploration.

© Great Source. Permission is granted to copy this page.

Poem 1: "Make it Go Away!"

Delete

Delet

Dele

Del

De

D

Poem 2: "Make a Wish"

```
                          J

      o                 ki
                                      p.

H       p,      S       p, and                    um
```

Shape It or Word It?

The following examples are two beginnings to concrete poems. The first example has a presentation idea but no words yet—just a title. The second has words but needs a presentation idea. Select one of these examples to work on as a way of practicing the two important elements of concrete poetry. Work with a partner—and have fun.

Choice #1: "No Boots in the House!"

Choice #2: Untitled (so far)

Everybody says how beautiful fall leaves are

With their red, orange, yellow, and brown.

They're more beautiful in

someone else's yard or a city park.

If you have to rake them,

they can become remarkably ugly. So . . .

If YOU want to "Oooh" and "Ahhh" over leaves,

just grab a rake and meet me at

123 SW Oak Street.

Where the heck are you and your rake,

oh mighty leaf lover?

Share and Compare

Share your concrete poems in a writing circle. Notice how words and presentation work together in each example.

A Writer's Questions

How do you feel about poetry? What is your previous experience with other forms of poetry? Does this form—concrete poetry—seem different from other types of poetry you have read or written? How?

Presentation Matters

In this part of the lesson, you will create your own concrete poem from the ground up, so to speak. How you start is up to you. You might choose to begin with

- words or word-play (look back at Examples 1, 2, and 3).

- a visual—a picture, outline, or geometric shape.

Visualize your poem hanging in an art gallery. Your readers are standing in front of it, soaking it all up. Here are some things for you to think about as you work.

- Hand lettering—big or small or varied? Caps or lower case?

- Shapes—will you build words into shapes or draw a sketch and then add the words, as with the boot poem?

- Exaggeration—repeating words, repeating letters, or exaggerating shapes

- Design—guiding the readers' eyes around the page

- Plain talk—good concrete poems often talk to you. They capture bits and pieces of actual speech.

HINT: Think of a small topic, something on your mind right now. It could be a remark someone made, something you've noticed, or some small thing that bothers you or makes you happy. Keep it simple. Keep it little and focused. (*World Peace* is pretty big. *Smiling* is more manageable.)

Name _____ Date _____

Sample Paper 19

Score for Sentence Fluency _____

Chocolate and the Witch's Curse

If you are one of the thousands of people who love chocolate so much that people call you a chocoholic, you might think you are paying more for your chocolate bars these days (or any chocolate for that matter), and in fact, you are most definitely right, but the reason might not be due to the first cause you think of. Chocolate, which used to be one of the least expensive treats you could buy now it is one of the most expensive. There is a reason for the cost increase and it's not just because the chocolate makers are raising their prices in order to make more money off the thousands of people who have chocolate addictions (you are not the only one!).

The true source of the trouble comes from a thing called witch's broom fungus which attacks the cacao bean, which is the source of chocolate, and turns the inside of the bean into a kind of mush. The cacao farmers have invented a kind of fungus of their own that attacks the witch's broom fungus except that the witch's broom fungus spreads so fast that the new fungus can't get rid of it fast enough to save very many of the cacao plants so it continues to spread.

A lot of the cocoa beans used for chocolate grow in South America, and that is where the largest cocoa bean plantations in the world can be found, so unless something can be done to stop the witch's broom fungus altogether, you can expect to keep paying more and more for your favorite chocolate bar. Scientists are not hopeful of finding a cure anytime soon, unfortunately.

Sources

Nicholas P. Money, _The Triumph of the Fungi._ New York, NY: Oxford University Press, 2007.

Money, Nicholas P. _Carpet Monsters and Killer Spores._ New York, NY, Oxford University Press, published in 2004.

http://www.oardc.ohio-state.edu/cocoa/witchbrm.htm

http://www.invasive.org/browse/subimages.cfm?sub=4881

http://www.ars.usda.gov/is/AR/archive/nov99/cacao1199.htm

Sample Paper 20
Score for Sentence Fluency _____

Spiders

Remember the old nursery rhyme about Little Miss Muffet—the one who leaped from her tuffet and took off on a run because a spider "sat down beside her"? Well, Muffet wasn't the only one to react that way. The average human yells or jumps anytime a spider suddenly wiggles up a nearby wall or dangles from an invisible dragline just inches from his or her nose. Our first instinct is to put as much distance as possible between ourselves and spiders, but it turns out that's harder than we thought. Some scientists suggest that as we go about our lives, we are never more than twelve feet from a spider! Even though the majority of spiders are very small, their eight fast moving legs, their bulbous shape, and their sticky webs all work together to strike fear into human hearts.

Many people kill spiders on sight—or call upon a brave friend or family member to dispatch the "intruder." Are we overreacting? Almost certainly. Most spider species are harmless to humans and, in fact, many are actually beneficial.

The domestic funnel weavers, like many of their spider relatives, should be honored for their work as exterminators. When these spiders are around, other kinds of creepy crawlies seem to disappear. On average, a spider consumes more than a hundred insects per year. They don't want to bother people; they just go where the food is—and that happens to be where people hang out. Face it: people attract insects.

Spider webs have been put to great use, too. Many years ago, healers discovered that webs could stop wounds from bleeding. (Specialists in wilderness survival still use this technique.) Webs are stronger, ounce for ounce, than steel, and are sometimes used in fishing nets. But the most useful thing of all may surprise you. It's the spiders' venom.

The Chilean tarantula is not only venomous; it's also particularly scary looking—large and hairy. When you're hoping to be rescued, this isn't the face you want to see. You might be more welcoming if you knew this spider could save your life. Here's how it works. When the cells in the heart stretch, it can cause the heart's rhythm to become irregular. The venom of the Chilean tarantula contains a protein that seems to prevent this swelling. Though more research is needed before people routinely take poison as a medicine, it's encouraging (and pretty amazing) to think that a spider's venom could actually save lives.

If humans are going to live in such close contact with spiders, we need to overcome our fear. We could start by having a little appreciation for all the pesky insects they eat—and the human lives they could save. Think about this the next time you are tempted to step on a spider—or just run away like Little Miss Muffet. Sit on your tuffet, relax, and say, "Another hundred down—keep up the good work! And hey, could I borrow part of that web . . . "

Sources

Baker, Lois. "Chilean Tarantula Venom." *Bio-Medicine.* 13 Oct. 2009 < http://news.bio-medicine.org/biology-news-2/Chemical-from-venom-of-Chilean-tarantula-could-aid-treatment-of-heart-attack--other-major-diseases-11512-1/>.

"Common US Spiders." Spiderz Rule! October 13, 2009 <http://www.spiderzrule.com/commonspidersusa.htm>.

Foelix, Rainer F. *Biology of Spiders.* New York, NY: Oxford University Press, 1996.

2001. Herbert W. Levi, *Spiders and Their Kin.* New York, NY: St. Martin's Press.

Complete Guide to Insects and Spiders *by Jinny Johnson.* London, UK: Book Sales, Inc, published in 2009.

Article from Bio-Medicine link: Chemical From Venom of Chilean Tarantula Could Aid Treatment of Heart Attack, Other Major Diseases by Lois Baker, May 15, 2000

Revising Checklist for Sentence Fluency

☐ I read this aloud. It's smooth and easy on the ear. The writing really *flows!*

☐ I <u>underlined</u> sentence beginnings (first three to four words) to check for variety.

☐ MANY sentences begin in different ways—with words that connect ideas. OR . . .

☐ I highlighted beginnings that could use revision.

☐ Some of my sentences are long and flowing, combining several ideas. Others are short and snappy.

☐ I checked for sentence problems. As needed to revise, I:

⎯⎯ combined some choppy sentences to make one smooth sentence.

⎯⎯ got rid of run-ons.

⎯⎯ got rid of fragments I did not *mean* to write.

⎯⎯ rewrote sentences that did not sound as fluent as I wanted them to.

☐ IF I used dialogue, I read it out loud to make sure it sounded like real conversation.

☐ ⎯⎯⎯⎯⎯⎯⎯⎯⎯⎯⎯⎯⎯⎯⎯⎯ rated my writing for Sentence Fluency:

1	2	3	4	5	6

☐ I used punctuation (and perhaps italics or ALL CAPS) to make sure readers would read my writing with *just* the right inflection.

Note When it comes to checking fluency, *nothing* takes the place of reading aloud. Remember: Just because a sentence is grammatically correct, that's no sign it's fluent and beautiful. You may need to write a sentence three or four ways to discover what makes it sing. Did you do that?

Student Rubric for Ideas

6
- My main message or story is clear and will hold your attention.
- I know this topic well and take readers on a journey of discovery.
- I include intriguing details a reader will notice and remember.
- My writing makes a point—or focuses on a clearly defined message.

5
- My main message or story is interesting and easy to understand.
- I share important information—and tell enough to give a full picture.
- My paper contains many interesting details.
- I narrow my topic enough to give readers an in-depth look at my subject.

4
- A reader can identify my main idea or make sense of my story.
- I have enough information for a first draft, but more would help.
- My writing includes a few interesting details. Readers might want more.
- I think I need to narrow my topic a little. I'm trying to cover too much.

3
- A reader can guess what my main idea is.
- I know enough to start—then I have to make things up.
- My details are general, things many readers already know.
- My topic feels way too BIG. I can't cover everything.

2
- A reader might have trouble figuring out the main message.
- The story or message isn't really clear in my mind. I just write to fill the page.
- I repeat things—or stop when I run out of things to say.
- I bounce from topic to topic—or list thoughts at random.

1
- I put my first thoughts on paper, but it's not a story—yet!
- I'm still figuring out my topic.

Student Rubric for Conventions and Presentation

6
- A reader will have to look hard to find errors in my writing!
- I edited carefully, reading silently and aloud. This is ready to publish.
- I used conventions to bring out the meaning and voice.
- My presentation has eye appeal and makes information easy to find.

5
- A careful reader might find minor errors—but nothing serious.
- It *might* need a few touchups, but it's *almost* ready to publish.
- My conventions support meaning and voice.
- My presentation makes important information stand out.

4
- Errors are noticeable, but they won't slow readers down.
- I need to go over this one more time, reading aloud as I edit.
- My conventions support the message and make reading fairly easy.
- My presentation is OK—it draws attention to key points.

3
- Readers might notice the errors more than the message!
- This writing needs *a lot* of editing.
- Mistakes could puzzle readers or force them to read some things twice.
- I need to work on presentation. Readers can't tell what to focus on.

2
- Parts of this are not edited at all. Mistakes jump right out!
- I need to go over this line-by-line, pencil in hand, reading aloud.
- Readers will need to "edit" as they read—that should be *my* job!
- I did not think about presentation yet.

1
- Mistakes make this hard to read, even for me.
- I have not done any editing yet—I'm not sure how to begin.
- Even if they read it two times, I'm not sure readers will get the message.
- I need help with editing and presentation.

Student Rubric for Organization

6
- Everything connects in some way to my MAIN message or story line.
- My paper is easy to follow—even with a quick reading. It has some twists and turns to make reading interesting!
- The lead is striking and will pull readers right in.
- The conclusion is original. I want to leave my readers thinking.

5
- I stay focused on the discussion or story all the way through.
- You can easily follow my "trail of thought."
- You'll like my lead—and it will hook you.
- My conclusion is satisfying. It wraps up the discussion or story.

4
- I may have wandered here and there—but I think you'll see a connection.
- I think you can follow this pretty easily.
- My lead sets things up. It kicks off the story or discussion.
- My ending wraps things up.

3
- I can see that I wandered in spots. This isn't always easy to follow.
- Or—maybe I needed more surprises! Readers could tell exactly what was coming!
- I have a lead—it could be more exciting.
- I have a conclusion. It's probably one you have heard before.

2
- I jumped from topic to topic. This is really hard to follow, even for me.
- This writing is like a messy closet! I need to move some things—or toss some out.
- I need a new lead.
- I need a new conclusion, too.

1
- I just wrote to get something on paper.
- Nothing goes with anything else. Don't look for a pattern!
- I didn't know how to begin.
- I didn't know how or when to stop, either.

Student Rubric for Voice

6
- This is ME. You can hear my voice in every line.
- A reader would *love* sharing this aloud.
- This topic matters deeply to me. I said exactly what I felt and thought.
- I wanted to reach readers—to make them feel the way I feel.

5
- This voice sounds like me. It doesn't blend in with others.
- I think some readers would share this writing aloud.
- Reading this writing will convince you I care about my topic.
- This voice fits my purpose and will get readers involved.

4
- I think my voice stands out from many others.
- There are some good moments to share.
- I care about this topic. I think that comes through in many parts.
- I think my voice will speak to many readers.

3
- I hear my voice in *parts* of this.
- With a little work, parts would be ready to share.
- I tried to sound excited, but I couldn't do it all the time.
- This voice won't reach all readers.

2
- This voice blends with many others. There's barely a whisper of ME.
- I don't feel ready to share this writing—yet.
- I need a topic I know and care more about.
- I'm still figuring out my purpose and who my readers are.

1
- There is nothing in this writing to make it mine.
- There's no reason to share this aloud.
- I don't have any strong feelings about this topic.
- I wrote what I had to write to finish the assignment.

Student Rubric for Word Choice

6
- You'll want to highlight memorable words and phrases.
- Lively verbs give my writing energy.
- Sensory details put readers right at the scene.
- You won't find clutter. Every word counts!

5
- My words are clear. I found *my own way* to say things.
- I used many strong verbs.
- I used sensory details in the right spots.
- There's little or no clutter.

4
- My words are used correctly.
- I used *some* strong verbs—and some adjectives.
- I used some sensory details—if they fit.
- Sometimes I repeated things or used words I didn't need.

3
- I used too many general words—or the wrong words.
- I need more verbs—or fewer modifiers!
- I need more sensory details. (Or I used TOO many!)
- It's wordy, repetitious, or overwritten.

2
- I used the first words I thought of.
- Most of my verbs are *is, are, was, were.* No real action!
- I told about things you *see*—but no *sounds, smells, feelings,* or *tastes.*
- It's wordy—or else I did not say enough.

1
- It was hard to find the right words. I did not know what to write.
- I wasn't sure how to use verbs.
- My writing doesn't help you picture things.
- I need more words—or different words.

Student Rubric for Sentence Fluency

6
- My writing is smooth and easy to read on the first try.
- Sentences differ in length and begin in ways that show how ideas connect.
- You can read this expressively to bring out every ounce of voice.
- If I used dialogue, it's so real you can perform it like a play.

5
- My writing flows smoothly. No bumps or sudden stops!
- Sentences differ in length and structure.
- It's easy to make this paper sound fluent and smooth.
- If I used dialogue, it sounds like real conversation.

4
- My writing is easy to read with a little practice.
- There's enough variety to make sentences interesting.
- With a little effort, you can make this writing sound fairly fluent.
- If I used dialogue, it's pretty realistic.

3
- Some parts are smooth—others are choppy or rambling.
- Too many sentences start the same way or are the same length.
- To read this smoothly, you need to rehearse—and pay attention.
- If I used dialogue, it needs work.

2
- Choppy sentences, run-ons, or other problems make reading slow.
- I use the same sentence patterns over and over. I might have fragments I didn't want.
- To read this aloud, prepare to "smooth over" some bumpy spots.
- I didn't use dialogue. Or else I couldn't make it sound real.

1
- This is hard to read. I'm not sure all my "sentences" are really sentences.
- It's hard to tell where my sentences begin and end.
- Words or punctuation could be missing. Readers need to fill these in.
- I didn't try to write any dialogue.